Bloom's Modern Critical Interpretations

Bloom's Modern Critical Interpretations

Aldous Huxley's
BRAVE NEW WORLD

Edited and with an introduction by
Harold Bloom
Sterling Professor of the Humanities
Yale University

CHELSEA HOUSE
PUBLISHERS
A Haights Cross Communications Company
Philadelphia

Printed and bound in the United States of America
10 9 8 7 6 5 4 3 2 1

Library of Congress Cataloging-in-Publication Data
Brave New World / Harold Bloom, editor; Aaron Tillman, consulting editor
        p. cm — (Modern critical interpretations)
Includes bibliographical references and index.
    ISBN 0-7910-7049-2
    1. Huxley, Aldous, 1894–1963. Brave new world. 2. Dystopias in literature. I. Bloom,
Harold. II. Tillman, Aaron. III. Series.
    PR6015.U9 B6724 2002
    823'.912—dc21

                                                              2002007535

Chelsea House Publishers
1974 Sproul Road, Suite 400
Broomall, PA 19008-0914

http://www.chelseahouse.com

Contributing Editor: Aaron Tillman

Cover design by Terry Mallon

Layout by EJB Publishing Services

Contents

Editor's Note

My Introduction briefly considers the tragedy of the Savage, *Brave New World's* unique Shakespearean.

William M. Jones nominates *Othello* as the dominant influence upon Huxley's dystopia, after which Peter Bowering finds the disaster of the Savage to have tragic inevitability.

To Harold H. Watts, *Brave New World* is an aesthetic success, avoiding Huxley's essayistic tendencies, while Jerome Meckier contrasts the book's satiric meaning to the "compensating dream" of Huxley's *Island*.

George Woodcock sees *Brave New World* as completing the vision of *Antic Hay* and *Point Counter Point*, after which Philip Thody sketches some biographical backgrounds.

In Robert S. Baker's view, the historical dialectics of the Marquis de Sade are crucial at the close of *Brave New World*, while Peter Edgerly Firchow studies the literary allusiveness of the book.

Robert S. Baker returns with an account of psychology in Huxley's Dystopia, after which, in another return, George Woodcock gives his final estimate of *Brave New World*.

June Deery concludes this volume as she confronts gender, and its problems, in the novel.

Introduction

In his "Foreword" to a 1946 edition of *Brave New World* (1931), Aldous Huxley expressed a certain regret that he had written the book when he was an amused, skeptical aesthete rather than the transcendental visionary he had since become. Fifteen years had brought about a world in which there were "only nationalistic radicals of the right and nationalistic radicals of the left," and Huxley surveyed a Europe in ruins after the completion of the Second World War. Huxley himself had found refuge in what he always was to call "the Perennial Philosophy," the religion that is "the conscious and intelligent pursuit of man's Final End, the unitive knowledge of the immanent Tao or Logos, the transcendent godhead or Brahman." As he sadly remarked, he had given his protagonist, the Savage, only two alternatives: to go on living in the Brave New World whose God is Ford (Henry), or to retreat to a primitive Indian village, more human in some ways, but just as lunatic in others. The poor Savage whips himself into the spiritual frenzy that culminates with his hanging himself. Despite Huxley's literary remorse, it seems to me just as well that the book does not end with the Savage saving himself through a mystical contemplation that murmurs "That are Thou" to the Ground of All Being.

A half-century after Huxley's "Foreword," *Brave New World* is at once a bit threadbare, considered strictly as a novel, and more relevant than ever in the era of genetic engineering, virtual reality, and the computer hypertext. Cyberpunk science fiction has nothing to match Huxley's outrageous inventions, and his sexual prophesies have been largely unfulfilled. Whether the Third Wave of a Gingrichian future will differ much from Huxley's *Brave New World* seems dubious to me. A new technology founded almost entirely upon information rather than production, at least for the elite, allies Mustapha Mond and Newt Gingrich, whose orphanages doubtless can be geared to the bringing up of Huxley's "Bokanovsky groups." Even Huxley's

1

intimation that "marriage licenses will be sold like dog licenses, good for a period of twelve months," was being seriously considered in California a few years ago. It is true that Huxley expected (and feared) too much from the "peaceful" uses of atomic energy, but that is one of his few failures in secular prophesy. The God of the Christian Coaltion may not exactly be Our Ford, but he certainly is the God whose worship assures the world without end of Big Business.

Rereading *Brave New World* for the first time in several decades, I find myself most beguiled by the Savage's passion for Shakespeare, who provides the novel with much more than its title. Huxley, with his own passion for Shakespeare, would not have conceded that Shakespeare could have provided the Savage with an alternative to a choice between an insane utopia and barbaric lunacy. Doubtless, no one ever has been saved by reading Shakespeare, or by watching him performed, but Shakespeare, more than any other writer, offers a possible wisdom, as well as an education in irony and the powers of language. Huxley wants his Savage to be a victim or scapegoat, quite possibly for reasons that Huxley himself never understood. *Brave New World*, like Huxley's earlier and better novels *Antic Hay* and *Point Counter Point*, is still a vision of T. S. Elliot's Waste Land, of a world without authentic belief and spiritual values. The author of *Heaven and Hell* and the anthologist of the *Perennial Philosophy* is latent in *Brave New World*, whose Savage dies in order to help persuade Huxley himself that he needs a reconciliation with the mystical Ground of All Being.

WILLIAM M. JONES

The Iago of Brave New World

The first half of Aldous Huxley's *Brave New World* is devoted almost entirely to the presentation of a society in which the only major freedom is a sexual one, a society built entirely on Community, Identity, Stability. Communal security has replaced all individual freedom. Ford-Freud has replaced God, and all the crosses have become T's. As Huxley is presenting this society to his reader, however, he is also preparing his plot structure. Eventually Lenina Crowne and Bernard Marx take a vacation to a New Mexico reservation together. There another society is presented, a primitive tribal one similar to that of the Brave New World in its emphasis on physical sensation and community. Their religious ceremony, in which a member of the tribe is beaten, is, in its basic urge, similar to the Solidarity Service of the Brave New World. And both societies demand total conformity.

Within this world is one person who does not belong to either. John Savage, as the son of an exile from the Brave New World, is not accepted by the primitive community. But, as the only one who has read Shakespeare, he is not suited to the Brave New World either. The Savage's knowledge of Shakespeare, which differentiates him from the other characters, makes him useful to Huxley as the plot-mover in the second half of the book.

When Lenina and Bernard return from their visit to the New Mexico reservation, they bring with them John Savage and his mother. The second

From *The Western Humanities Review* 15, 3. © 1961 by *The Western Humanities Review*.

half of the book then utilizes the device of introducing a stranger into a new society. This stranger, however, is not, as most outsiders are, an exact equivalent of our own society; he is part savage, part Brave New World, and part Shakespeare. As a Shakespearean he plays his part as deceived lover, and as Shakespearean he judges the society. From his first glimpse of Lenina, when he blushes and quotes Miranda, How beauteous mankind is! to his last condemnation of her, Fry, lechery, fry! he is guided by Shakespearean attitudes and quotations.

Underneath the attitudes and quotations is also a Shakespearean construction. Huxley prepares the reader for this construction by giving a detailed account of the feelie that Lenina and John see on their first date: in a helicopter accident a big Negro receives a concussion that destroys his conditioning. He develops an exclusive passion for a blonde, she resists, he kidnaps her, keeps her alone in a helicopter, she is rescued by three young men, the Negro is sent to an Adult Reconditioning Center, and the film ends happily with the blonde becoming the mistress of all her rescuers.

Later, when Lenina attempts to kiss John, he recalls this feelie with horror. And almost at the conclusion of the book, he questions the World Controller about the movie: 'Why don't you let them see *Othello* instead?' The obvious similarities between the movie and *Othello* suggest this play rather than some other. As a matter of fact, through his whole conversation with the Controller, the play the Savage refers to most often is *Othello*. 'Goats and monkeys!' the Savage says, quoting *Othello* to show his contempt for the feelie-viewers. And the World Controller says that ' ... our world is not the same as Othello's world. You can't make flivvers without steel and you can't make tragedies without social instability.'

But the irony of the situation is that Huxley has made the feelie plot show us the Brave New World's version of *Othello*, and he has built his own plot on the outline of *Othello* as well. We are given in the second half of the book two variations on a theme by Shakespeare. Huxley's whole development denies the statement made by the Controller: ' ... if it were really like *Othello* nobody could understand it, however new it might be. And if it were new, it couldn't possibly be like *Othello*.'

Shakespeare's *Othello* presents an outsider who marries a beautiful girl and carries her off against the wishes of her father. A villain, Iago, poisons the mind of the outsider against his wife, suggesting that all Venetian women are promiscuous and unfaithful. The outsider, in a fit of rage, murders his wife. The Brave New World's *Othello* is an outsider, the Negro, who carries off a girl against the wishes of society. Society, however, is able to recondition the outsider so that all is well. Huxley's *Othello* character is an outsider who loves a girl, but whose mind is poisoned against her, not by an individual villain, but by the entire society which has produced her. From our own point of view, the entire society that produced Lenina is the Iago. That society's stability has made true affection impossible, and in so doing has contributed to the tragedy which its Controller felt was impossible.

Huxley's structure, however, makes Shakespeare himself, whose whole ethic differed from that of the Brave New World, serve as Iago. Shakespeare kept John Savage from a satisfactory relationship with the girl he loved, just as Iago kept Othello from Desdemona. Othello was duped by lying Iago, who corrupted his mind against the purity of Desdemona. In a society such as Shakespeare's, where purity and virtuous living were respected by all, the disturbing influence would be an Iago. In the Brave New World, where the Desdemona character Lenina is praised for her promiscuity and where the characteristics of Shakespeare's Desdemona would be frowned upon, the Iago character becomes a disturbing influence of another sort. It is Shakespeare who causes the Savage to fail in his adjustment to the new world. In both *Othello* and *Brave New World*, the Othello character has the same basic attitudes. He is a just and honest man duped. In an honest society, the villain, therefore, would be evil; in a perverted one the villain would be, in our eyes, good.

John Savage, the Othello character, is the pivotal one. He parallels Othello, whereas all else in the novel is the reverse of the play. The Desdemona of the Brave New World is unchaste, as her perverted society demands, and the Iago of the Brave New World is not a villain, but the man an upright society regards as one of its leading representatives: Shakespeare. In a perverted society, the good of one society becomes, naturally, the evil of the other.

Only by recognizing, either consciously or unconsciously, this *Othello* pattern, can the reader accept the conclusion of the novel. After two chapters devoted to a discussion of art, science, and religion, two main characters are sent to an island for the hopelessly unconditionable, and John Savage is left to solitude within the new society. Why Huxley did not end the book happily by permitting the Savage to accompany the two can be answered only in terms of *Othello*. Huxley has been building to a tragedy with a new Othello, one incapable of becoming one-eyed in a one-eyed society, one who refuses to play insane to seem sane in an insane society. The Savage's tragedy, like Othello's, is that of a man deceived by himself as well as by a villain. At the moment when Lenina comes forward in true affection, two tears rolled down her cheeks, the Savage's own lack of control causes him to rush upon her and kill her.

Huxley has prepared us for the depth of tragedy here by once more setting up an *Othello* parallel. Earlier the Savage has protested against the new world's happiness: 'But the tears are necessary. Don't you remember what Othello said? If after every tempest came such calms, may the winds blow till they have wakened death.' Lenina's tears show her return to sanity at the moment the Savage, like Othello, gives way to momentary madness. Without the *Othello* parallels the conclusion might seem vaguely pessimistic, but with the echo of *Othello* behind it this conclusion takes on the positive power of deep tragedy: the Othello character destroying at the moment of potential fulfillment. After this temporary loss of control comes the terrible enlightenment that precedes the suicide. Both Othello and the Savage have been forced to murder and suicide by a villain, one a soulless Iago, one an honest Shakespeare.

At the end of the story Huxley's reader feels the same sense of tragic loss that the reader of *Othello* feels. Here were men of promise duped by disturbing influences. In the enlightened society of the new world Shakespeare brought John Savage to destruction by revealing truth to him; in *Othello* Iago brought the destruction by revealing lies. Huxley has wisely chosen the Shakespearean play that would best fit his Brave New World and has built upon it while his characters are protesting against it.

PETER BOWERING

Brave New World *(1932)*

Huxley has been compared to H. G. Wells as a popularizer of scientific ideas and as a revolutionary and prophetic writer. Both certainly can be considered as prophets in their own right, but if Wells is the prophet of scientific optimism Huxley is without doubt its prophet of gloom. In his utopia of the early twenties *Men Like Gods*, Wells depicts a modern world-state in which private ownership, religious worship and parental control have been replaced by socialism, scientific humanism and education by the state, where eugenics and birth control have produced a society that nurtures freedom and tolerance. All the elements of control exercised by the Wellsian world-state are to be found in *Brave New World*, but whereas Wells sees technological progress leading to a new millennium—a race of athletic chemists and mathematical physicists, Huxley envisages the birth of a scientific dictatorship in which the last traces of individuality have been ruthlessly stamped out. In *The Shape of Things to Come* Wells dismisses Huxley's view as an alarmist fantasy; he accepts scientific totalitarianism as a necessary evil which will ultimately wither away as man becomes more enlightened. Accordingly, at the hypothetical conference of Mégève set in the year 2059, his guardians of the future world-state dismiss themselves with the proclamation that the need for repressions and disciplines has passed, and that everyone is free to express himself to the limit of his

From *Aldous Huxley: A Study of the Major Novels.* © 1968 by Peter Bowering.

potentialities. This act of benevolence on the part of the ruling guardians and the revolution of the educational élite which leads up to it would have seemed to Huxley highly improbable. He would have agreed with Wells that under a scientific dictator 'education will really work' but, as he points out, in *Brave New World Revisited* the result will be 'that most men and women will grow up to love their servitude and will never dream of revolution'; he concludes that 'there seems to be no good reason why a thoroughly scientific dictatorship should ever be overthrown' (ch. xii). *Brave New World* is the portrait of such a dictatorship.

In the office of the World Controller for Western Europe lies a copy of 'My Life and Work, by Our Ford'. It is no coincidence that 'Our Ford' is both the patron saint and prophet of Huxley's new world-state. 'Fordism', he wrote in a contemporary essay, 'demands that we should sacrifice the animal man (and along with the animal large portions of the thinking, spiritual man) not indeed to God, but to the Machine. There is no place in the factory, or in that larger factory which is the modern industrialized world, for animals on the one hand, or for artists, mystics, or even, finally, individuals on the other. Of all the ascetic religions Fordism is that which demands the cruellest mutilations of the human psyche—demands the cruellest mutilations and offers the smallest spiritual returns' ('The Puritan', *Music at Night*). Fordism, the philosophy of applied science and industrialism, is the religion of *Brave New World*. By the double process of genetic manipulation and post-natal conditioning the World Controllers have succeeded in producing a race which loves its servitude, a race of standardized machine-minders for standardized machines who will never challenge their authority. The animal, thinking and spiritual man has been sacrificed in his entirety.

At the beginning of *Brave New World*, the Director of Hatcheries and Conditioning describes Bokanovsky's process, whereby 'an average of nearly eleven thousand brothers and sisters in a hundred and fifty batches of identical twins' could be produced from a single ovary, as one of the major instruments of social stability. The problem of selective breeding has been a favourite subject of scientific speculation since the beginning of the century: the scientist in Lowes Dickinson's *A Modern Symposium* (first published in 1905) affirms that 'it may be desirable for government to undertake the complete regulation of marriage'. And Huxley concluded, following Wells, that general progress was only possible upon two conditions: that the heritable qualities of the population be improved and that the population be reduced. Eugenic reform, however, raises its own problems: in a society of superior individuals only a chosen few could be permitted to make full use of their powers because no society provides openings for more than a limited number of superior people. Wells solved this problem by allowing his utopian inhabitants to rule and be ruled, to do highbrow and lowbrow work in turns, but Huxley was characteristically sceptical of such a solution; governments only rule, effectively because most people are not very intelligent, dread responsibility and desire nothing better than to be told what to do. The World Controllers of *Brave New World* held similar views and created a highly stable, differentiated society by means of ectogenesis, in which both eugenics and dysgenics were practised systematically at the same time:

> In one set of bottles biologically superior ova, fertilized by biologically superior sperm, were given the best possible pre-natal treatment and were finally decanted as Betas, Alphas and even Alpha Pluses. In another, much more numerous set of bottles, biologically inferior ova, fertilized by biologically inferior sperm, were subjected to the Bokanovsky Process (ninety-six identical twins out of a single egg) and treated pre-natally with alcohol and other protein poisons. The creatures finally decanted were almost sub-human; but they were capable of performing unskilled work.... (*Brave New World Revisited*, ch. ii)

Those decanted as Alphas and Alpha Pluses were destined for a higher education (Eton was reserved exclusively for Alpha caste boys and girls) and posts of responsibility; while the lower and more numerous castes manned the benches of industry, where each process was carried out as far as possible by a single Bokanovsky group. By controlled ectogenesis and the Bokanovsky Process the population of the planet was fixed at two thousand million inhabitants with only ten thousand names between them.

The Bokanovsky Process and pre-natal treatment of the embryos insured that the future inhabitants of *Brave New World* were decanted as socialized human beings, but this was merely a beginning. After birth infants were subjected to an intensive course of behaviourist and hypnopaedic conditioning, primarily designed to make their minds endorse the already predestined judgment of their bodies. As the Director of Hatcheries explained, 'that is the secret of happiness and virtue—liking what you've got to do. All conditioning aims at that: making people like their unescapable social destiny' (ch. i). In John B. Watson's classic study of behaviourism, the American psychologist describes techniques for establishing conditioned reflexes in infants. One series of experiments shows how an eleven-month-old baby, who is perfectly at ease with tame white rodents, can be conditioned to a fear response, simply by striking a steel bar with a hammer every time he approaches the proximity of the animals. After this has been repeated seven times, the mere sight of a rodent or any related animal is sufficient to produce intense fear and dismay.[1] In the Neo-Pavlovian Conditioning Rooms at the Infant Nurseries, eight-month-old, khaki-clad Delta babies are treated by identical techniques: encouraged to approach bowls of roses and brightly-coloured nursery quartos, they are subjected simultaneously to the loud ringing of alarm bells and electric shocks. After two hundred repetitions, books and loud noises, flowers and electric shocks are indissolubly wedded: "They'll grow up with what the psychologists used to call an 'instinctive' hatred of books and flowers. Reflexes unalterably conditioned, They'll be safe from books and botany all their lives' (ch. ii).

In *Brave New World Revisited* Huxley discusses Wetterstrand's successful hypnotic treatment of sleeping children and concludes that, under proper conditions, hypnopaedia or sleep teaching actually works about as well as hypnosis. The Controllers of *Brave New World* have taken full advantage of the fact. The Director of Hatcheries called hypnopaedia 'the greatest moralizing and socializing force of all time'. Wordless conditioning had its value, but it was relatively crude and limited when it came to the finer distinctions; for that there had to be words but words without reason. Therefore part of the moral education of Beta children consisted in 'lessons' in elementary class consciousness. While the children slept a voice under every pillow softly whispered:

> 'Alpha children wear grey. They work much harder than we do, because they're so frightfully clever. I'm really awfully glad I'm a Beta, because I don't work so hard. And then we are much better than the Gammas and Deltas. Gammas are stupid. They all wear green, and Delta children wear khaki. Oh no, I *don't* want to play with Delta children. And Epsilons are still worse. They're too stupid to be able ... (ch. ii)

Finally, as the Director sums up, 'the child's mind *is* these suggestions, and the sum of the suggestions is the child's mind. And not the child's mind only. The adult's mind too—all his life long' (ch. ii).

After ectogenesis and conditioning, Soma[2] was the most powerful instrument of authority in the hands of the Controllers of the World-State. Huxley had already speculated on the invention of a new drug, a more efficient and less harmful substitute for alcohol and cocaine; he considered that if he were a millionaire, he would endow a band of research workers to look for the ideal intoxicant. The rulers of *Brave New World*, with a similar object in mind, had subsidized two thousand pharmacologists and biochemists to search for the perfect drug. Soma was the product of six years research; euphoric, narcotic, pleasantly hallucinant, it had all the advantages of alcohol and none of the defects, but there the resemblance ended. To the inhabitants of Huxley's utopia the Soma habit was not a private vice but a political institution. The World Controllers encouraged the systematic drugging of their own citizens for the benefit of the state.

> The daily Soma ration was an insurance against personal maladjustment, social unrest and the spread of subversive ideas. Religion, Karl Marx declared, is the opium of the people. In the Brave New World this situation was reversed. Opium, or rather Soma, was the people's religion. Like religion, the drug had power to console and compensate, it called up visions of another, better world, it offered hope, strengthened faith and promoted charity. (*Brave New World Revisited*, ch. viii)

Huxley, comparing his novel with *1984*, observes that in the latter a strict code of sexual morality is imposed on the party hierarchy. The society of Orwell's fable is permanently at war and therefore aims to keep its subjects in a constant state of tension. A puritanical approach to sex is therefore a major instrument of policy. The World-State, however, of *Brave New World* is one in which war has been eliminated and the first aim of its rulers is to keep their subjects from making trouble. Together with Soma, sexual licence, made practical by the abolition of the family, is one of the chief means of guaranteeing the inhabitants against any kind of destructive or creative emotional tension. The appalling dangers of family life had first been pointed out by Our Ford or 'Our Freud, as, for some inscrutable reason, he chose to call himself whenever he spoke of psychological matters' (ch. iii). Once the world had been full of every kind of perversion from chastity to sadism; but the World Controllers had realized that an industrial civilization depended on self-indulgence. Chastity meant passion and neurasthenia, and passion and neurasthenia meant instability, which, in turn, meant a constant threat to civilization. Therefore life for the Brave New Worlders was made emotionally easy; in short, people were saved from having emotions at all. No one was allowed to love anyone too much; there were no temptations to resist, and if something unpleasant were to happen, there was always Soma. Legalized sexual freedom was made possible by every device known to applied science. Contraceptive precautions were prescribed by the regulations while years of 'intensive hypnopaedia and, from twelve to seventeen, Malthusian drill three times a week had made the taking of these precautions almost as automatic and inevitable as blinking' (ch. v).

Soma and licensed promiscuity would probably have been sufficient in themselves to prevent the Brave New Worlders from taking any active interest in the realities of the social and political situation; circuses, however, are a traditional aid to dictators, and the Controllers of the World-State were no exception. Instead of spending their leisure hours working out the practical implications of the theory of relativity, like their predecessors in *Men Like Gods*, Huxley's utopians were provided with a series of non-stop distractions guaranteed to ward off boredom and discourage idle speculation about the nature of things. Any frustrated religious instincts were provided for by the Ford's Day Solidarity Services, where, in a crude parody of the Holy Communion, dedicated Soma Tablets and the loving cup of ice-cream Soma were passed round. By these means the Controllers insured that the Brave New Worlders loved their servitude and never dreamt of revolution.

In *Brave New World* the imprisonment of the human spirit by science is almost complete; human values have totally disappeared, natural impulses allowed to atrophy until the inhabitants react like automata. Only in the remote Indian Reservation, which, owing to a poor climate and a lack of natural resources, has not been worth civilizing, have the normal values of humanity survived. There, surrounded by electrified fencing, some sixty thousand Indians and half-breeds still practise marriage, rear families and preserve the religious traditions of the past. One among them, John, is the natural born son of a Brave New Worlder, Linda, who had been left behind during one of the infrequent expeditions from outside. John, brought up as an Indian, taught to read Shakespeare and to listen to his mother's stories of the Other Place, is Huxley's device for introducing an outsider with relatively normal values into his world of scientifically conditioned inhabitants. (Wells used a similar device when he introduced the Earthlings into the utopia of *Men Like Gods*, although his intention was, of course, the exact opposite of Huxley's.) John, and through him, Shakespeare, becomes the symbol of the human spirit, opposed to Fordism and applied science:

> ... the Savage has the weakness and the strength of a personality not 'artificially made'. He wants to love, but to love for ever. He wants to work, but to work with effort and in the sweat of his brow. He wants to live, but to live dangerously. He wants to rejoice, but he wants also to suffer. He wants life with its fulness, but he wants also death with its tragedy. All the wonders of

material civilisation leave him cold, because he remembers that:
'*Ariel could put a girdle round the earth in forty minutes.*'[3]

Above all, he wants God, goodness and sin—he claims the right to be unhappy, to which the World-Controller adds the final ironic comment: 'Not to mention the right to grow old and ugly and impotent, the right to have syphilis and cancer; the right to have too little to eat; the right to be lousy; the right to live in a constant apprehension of what may happen tomorrow; the right to catch typhoid; the right to be tortured by unspeakable pains of every kind' (ch. xvii). The Savage claims them all; but, as the World Controller insists, the price of freedom is inordinately high. In the end, the Savage's resistance amounts to little more than an heroic gesture. He rejects the world which no longer seems brave or beauteous. The burden is inevitably too great; like Lypiatt, in his extremity, he has no other recourse but to end his life in a fit of despair.

At a first glance the Savage, with his insatiable desire for experience, appears as an embodiment of the 'life-worshipper's' creed. His peculiar blend of the primitive and the civilized points to Rampion's 'balanced opposites'; against this his '*penitente* ferocity', the savagery with which he greets Lenina's sensual advances, is far from the 'life-worshipper's' ideal. Whatever Huxley's intentions were, it would be unwise to push the equation too far. It is the Brave New Worlders who give John the title of the Savage, but it is important to note that the irony is double-edged. Humanity's last living representative owes his allegiance to a creed that is half fertility cult and half *penitente* ferocity. The Indians are far from being 'noble' and, if 'civilization is sterilization', savagery means goitre and flagellation. And John, in spite of his Shakespearean upbringing, is still very much a savage. As Huxley himself admitted, the choice lay 'between insanity on the one hand and lunacy on the other'—the insanity of the scientific utopia or the lunacy of the primitive cult (Foreword to *Brave New World*). The failure of the Savage to find a real alternative suggests, in spite of the many echoes of 'life worship', that Huxley was moving away from the doctrine of *Do What You Will*. There was as yet nothing to take its place and, although the introduction of Maine de Biran late in the novel anticipates a renewed interest in the life of the spirit, the contemplative solution still lay ahead. Thirty years later, in *Island*, Huxley was to offer a real alternative, another utopia, in which science and technology would be used not to enslave man but to further his salvation.

John, in his redemptive role, has two potential converts among the Brave New Worlders, Bernard Marx and Helmholtz Watson. Both are Alpha Pluses. The Alphas of the scientific society are all products of excessive cerebration: 'Adults intellectually and during working hours... Infants where feeling and desire are concerned'. The terms are familiar: this kind of 'unbalanced excess' is the typical defect of the 'scientific' character. Bernard, however, whose predicament recalls that of Philip Quarles, is something of an odd man out even among the Brave New Worlders. An Alpha Plus, he has the physique of a Gamma-Minus (it is said that alcohol had been put into his blood surrogate by mistake). His inadequacy nurtures a sense of revolt: but more important, Bernard's grievances are not merely anti-social; behind his revolt stems a genuine impulse to extend his range of feeling—to know what it would be like if he were not enslaved by his conditioning:

> On their way back across the Channel, Bernard insisted on stopping his propeller and hovering on his helicopter screws within a hundred feet of the waves...
>
> 'Look,' he commanded.
>
> 'But it's horrible', said Lenina, shrinking back from the window. She was appalled by the rushing emptiness of the night, by the black foam-flecked water heaving beneath them, by the pale face of the moon, so haggard and distracted among the hastening clouds. 'Let's turn on the radio. Quick.' She reached for the dialling knob on the dashboard and turned it at random...
>
> 'I want to look at the sea in peace', he said. 'One can't even look with that beastly noise going on.'
>
> 'But it's lovely. And I don't want to look.'
>
> 'But I do', he insisted. 'It makes me feel as though ...' he hesitated, searching for words with which to express himself, 'as though I were more *me*, if you see what I mean. More on my own, not so completely a part of something else. Not just a cell in the social body.' (ch. vi)

Bernard's problem, like that of Philip Quarles, is how to be an adult all the time, not just intellectually but with his senses as well. This is the 'life-worshipper's' problem—to achieve the harmony of Rampion's 'balanced opposites'.

Helmholtz Watson's sense of dissatisfaction springs, less plausibly, from having too much ability. This, like Bernard's physical defect, isolates him from his fellow men. A successful lecturer, an indefatigable lover and an Escalator-Squash champion, he has nevertheless realized that sport, women and communal activities are not enough. Bernard and Helmholtz are too conditioned to present a serious threat to the values of the Brave New World, but, together with John, they form a core of resistance within the deterministic society. John precipitates his friends into something approaching open revolt; the three are arrested and Bernard and Helmholtz duly sent into exile. The only positive result of John's bid for freedom is expressed in a moment of genuine affection when the three meet for the last time: 'There was a silence. In spite of their sadness—because of it, even; for their sadness was the symptom of their love for one another—the three young men were happy' (ch. xviii).

In a society where sexual licence has supplanted love, feelings of desire are virtually unknown. Both Bernard and Helmholtz try to make themselves more 'human' by practising self-denial. Bernard wants to examine the effect of arresting his impulses; Helmholtz finds the effects of abstinence worthwhile but exceedingly odd. For Bernard the process is little short of the rediscovery of free will. 'Thought' is still 'the slave of life' but, he concludes, the process appears to be reversible:

> A physical shortcoming could produce a kind of mental excess. The process, it seemed, was reversible. Mental excess could produce, for its own purposes, the voluntary blindness and deafness of deliberate solitude, the artificial impotence of asceticism. (ch. iv)

This is the first step to redemption; it denotes a crack in the iron-bound determinism which overshadowed the protagonists of *Point Counter Point*, and looks ahead to Anthony Beavis's discovery in *Eyeless in Gaza* that the conditioned reflexes could themselves be reconditioned.

By introducing Shakespeare to the World-State, the Savage brings the first taste of culture into a cultureless society. Following Ford's dictum that 'History is bunk', all the art and knowledge of the past has been suppressed—only a few pre-Fordian books remain locked in the safe in the World Controller's study. No one was encouraged to indulge in solitary amusements. When the Savage suggests *Othello* as an alternative to 'Three Weeks in a Helicopter', the Controller points out that no one would understand it. Tragedies depend on an environment which lacks social stability. Now, the world is stable:

> People are happy; they get what they want, and they never want what they can't get. They're well off, they're safe; they're never ill; they're not afraid of death; they're blissfully ignorant of

passion and old age; they're plagued with no mothers or fathers; they've got no wives, or children, or lovers to feel strongly about; they're so conditioned that they practically can't help behaving as they ought to behave. And if anything should go wrong, there's *soma*. (ch. xvi)

Othello is admittedly better than the feelies but a price must be paid for stability. The choice lay between happiness and what people used to call high art. The high art has been sacrificed; but, as the Controller admits, actual happiness never looks exciting and 'being contented has none of the glamour of a good fight against misfortune, none of the picturesqueness of a struggle with temptation, or a fatal overthrow by passion or doubt. Happiness is never grand' (ch. xvi).

To the Savage in his search for spiritual values, the brand of 'happiness' offered by the World-State is inevitably inadequate, and the death of Linda serves to emphasize the intrinsic nature of the conflict between two essentially incompatible ways of life. When Linda is brought back among the Brave New Worlders no one wishes to see her, ostensibly because she is not a real savage, but really because she has aged. At forty-four, she has lost her youth, and not one of the citizens of civilization can look on her without a feeling of nausea. In the World-State old age has been conquered and with it all the mental attitudes of senility. Men who in the old days would have spent their time in retirement, reading, thinking, and turning to religion, now work and make love. There is no rest from pleasure, not a moment to sit down and think. Preservation from disease and biochemical adjustments keep them permanently youthful until, at the age of sixty, they suddenly break down and death is immediate. In this world of youth the ageing Linda has no place and her return to civilization becomes, in effect, one prolonged Soma holiday. A few months later she lies in the special hospital for the dying, surrounded by every distraction that applied science can invent. The Savage's desire to be with her at the end defies all the conventions of the scientific society. Brave New Worlders have no close relationships; the individual as an individual has ceased to matter. Further, the act of dying has been stripped of all significance. Intensive conditioning from the age of eighteen months—every tot spent two mornings a week in a Hospital for the Dying; all the best toys were kept there, with special helpings of chocolate cream on death days—has robbed death of its terrors. Soma and synthetic melodies do the rest. The Savage, who sees death in a rather different light, tries to restore Linda to consciousness, but she is dreaming happily of Popé, her Indian lover.

He squeezed her limp hand almost with violence, as though he would force her to come back from this dream of ignoble pleasures, from these base and hateful memories—back into the present, back into reality; the appalling present, the awful reality—but sublime, but significant, but desperately important precisely because of the imminence of that which made them so fearful. (ch. xiv)

This is the first intimation of the importance which Huxley was to attach to the act of dying. In the last novels, holy living and holy dying become an integral part of Huxley's philosophy,[4] and death is seen as the culminating point of human experience. To the Brave New Worlders death has no more spiritual significance than life, and as such is merely an unpleasant termination to what is otherwise a state of unqualified contentment.

By abolishing old age and the fear of death, the rulers of *Brave New World* feel that they have not only eradicated spiritual values, but have further removed all need for God. The World Controller quotes Maine de Biran (one of the few surviving authors in his collection of pre-Fordian volumes) to prove his point:

... the religious sentiment tends to develop as we grow older; to develop because, as the passions grow calm, as the fancy and sensibilities are less excited and less excitable, our reason becomes less troubled in its working ... whereupon God emerges as from behind a cloud; our soul feels, sees, turns towards the source of all light; turns naturally and inevitably; for now that all that gave to the world of sensations its life and charm has begun to leak away from us ... we feel the need to lean on something that abides, something that will never play us false—a reality, an absolute and everlasting truth. Yes, we inevitably turn to God; for this religious sentiment is of its nature so pure, so delightful to the soul that experiences it, that it makes up to us for all our other losses. (ch. xvii)

For the citizens of the World-State there are no losses to compensate for; there is no need for a substitute for youthful desires when youthful desires remain to the end, therefore religious sentiment is rendered superfluous. And, if there is no need for God, then the values which human beings normally reverence are likewise irrelevant; self-denial and chastity, nobility and patience are also superfluous. There is no need for any civilized man to bear anything that is unpleasant. God and moral values are incompatible with machinery, scientific medicine and universal happiness.

In the World-State man has been enslaved by science, or as the hypnopaedic platitude puts it, 'science is everything'. But, while everything owes its origin to science, science itself has been paradoxically relegated to the limbo of the past along with culture, religion and every other worthwhile object of human endeavour. It is ironic that science, which has given the stablest equilibrium in history, should itself be regarded as a potential menace, and that all scientific progress should have been frozen since the establishment of the World-State. But it was Whitehead who said, in warning against the dangers inherent in the scientific method, 'A self-satisfied rationalism is in effect a form of anti-rationalism. It means an arbitrary halt at a particular set of abstractions'.[5] This is what has happened in *Brave New World*, where a self-satisfied rationalism has called an arbitrary halt at ectogenesis, behaviourism and hypnopaedia. The result is anti-rational in the extreme. The cause of this lies in the intrinsic nature of science itself. Wells foresaw a scientific utopia based on science as a love of truth, and knowledge for its own sake; in Huxley's utopia, science has degenerated into an instrument of power. Today it would seem that Huxley's vision is the truer one. The kind of knowledge that science provides inevitably extends man's power over the physical world. Science therefore can pursue knowledge for its own sake, as Wells envisaged; or alternatively it can pursue knowledge for the sake of power. In the twentieth century, science has increasingly become identified with the pursuit of power. Russell, commenting on this tendency, drew a similar conclusion when he noted that 'We may seek knowledge of an object because we love the object or because we wish to have power over it' and that 'The scientific society of the future ... is one in which the power impulse has completely overwhelmed the impulse of love.'[6] In *Brave New World* not only has the pursuit of all intuitive knowledge disappeared, but science itself has become incompatible with truth. Russell's summing-up which might well have served as a text for this novel, states: 'The scientific society in its pure form ... is incompatible with the pursuit of truth, with love, with art, with spontaneous delight, with every ideal that men have hitherto cherished ... It is not knowledge that is the source of these dangers. Knowledge is good and ignorance is evil ... Nor is it power in and for itself that is the source of danger. What is dangerous is power wielded for the sake of power, not power wielded for the sake of genuine good'.[7]

The epigraph to *Brave New World*, a quotation from Nicolas Berdiaeff, posed a question:

> Les utopies apparaissent comme bien plus réalisables qu'on ne le croyait autrefois. Et nous nous trouvons actuellement devant une question autrement angoissante: Comment éviter leur réalisation définitive?

Huxley's fable makes no attempt to provide an answer; however, in *Brave New World Revisited*, he returns to this point. Arguing the case for individual freedom, he emphasizes the importance of heredity in the life of the individual and society. Every individual is biologically unique and unlike other individuals. Freedom and tolerance are therefore necessary if human beings are to develop to their full potential. Many years earlier in *Beyond the Mexique Bay*, he had stressed the significance of 'freedom' in primitive societies:

> Man's biological success was due to the fact that he never specialized. Unfitted by his physique to do any one thing to perfection, he was forced to develop the means for doing everything reasonably well. Civilization reverses the evolutionary process. Primitives are men who have never succumbed to the suicidal ambition to resemble ants. Generalization—this is the great, the vitally important lesson they have to teach the specialists of the civilised world.

It follows that any education for freedom must stress 'the facts of human diversity and genetic uniqueness', together with 'the value of charity and compassion, based upon the old familiar fact, lately rediscovered by modern psychiatry—the fact that, whatever their mental and physical diversity, love is as necessary to human beings as food and shelter; and finally the value of intelligence, without which love is impotent and freedom unattainable' (*Brave New World Revisited*, ch. xi). As for society, the only way to avoid the threat of a future scientific utopia is to decentralize; science tends progressively to group men into larger and larger units with a proportionate loss of individual freedom—to counter this it is necessary to form small self-governing communities, freed from the restrictions of Big Business and Big Government, where people can work together as individuals and not as the embodiment of specialized functions. To persist on our present course is to invite disaster:

> When we think presumptuously that we are, or shall become in some future Utopian state, 'men like gods', then in fact we are in mortal danger of becoming devils, capable only (however exalted our 'ideals' may be, however beautifully worked out our plans and blue-prints) of ruining our world and destroying ourselves. ('Man and Reality', *Vedanta for the Western World*)

The triumph of humanism, Huxley prophesies, will prove the ultimate defeat of humanity.

NOTES

[1] *Behaviourism* (Chicago, 1959), pp. 159–64.
[2] The original Soma from which Huxley took the name of this hypothetical drug was an unknown plant used by the ancient Aryan invaders of India in one of the most solemn of their religious rites.
[3] M. D. Petre, *The Hibbert Journal*, xxxi (October 1932), p. 70.
[4] The deaths of Eustace Barnack and Lakshmi are central to the themes of *Time Must Have a Stop* and *Island*.
[5] *Science and the Modern World*, p. 250
[6] *The Scientific Outlook*, pp. 269–73.
[7] op. cit., p. 274.

HAROLD H. WATTS

Brave New World

At a time when Huxley was involved in his continuing periodical journalism and also in the editing of the letters of D. H. Lawrence, he published his great utopian novel, *Brave New World* (1932). The title comes from Shakespeare's *The Tempest*, where the innocent Miranda exclaims: "O wonder! / How many goodly creatures are there here! / How beauteous mankind is! O brave new world, / That has such people in't!" (Act V, scene 1). The lines in Shakespeare are sufficiently ironical since the "creatures" that arouse Miranda's admiration are mostly scoundrels. Huxley's use of the phrase deepens the irony, for his world of the future is one that much modern speculations hope will come to pass; yet the texture of his imagined world is nearer to nightmare than to heaven on earth.

Brave New World is, by common acceptance, Huxley's most celebrated book. From the fairly complex point of view towards Huxley's work that seems to be most just—that of considering each work by its esthetic success *and* its power to express aspects of the twentieth-century cultural situation— a kind of double but related judgment may be passed. As utopian fiction, *Brave New World* has great esthetic success; it fuses what one presently recognizes as the dangerous incompatibles of this form into a telling unity. And the novel is, just as interestingly, a notable record of uncertainties and hopes proper not only to Huxley but also to the era in which he writes; in

From *Aldous Huxley*. © 1969 by Twayne Publishers, Inc.

consequence, it can be used as a key to analysis of the times by persons who regard as somewhat irrelevant to their purpose questions of esthetic success. Both sorts of judgment must be explored. Furthermore, the novel must be seen as expressive of the developing opinions of Huxley himself.

I. *Utopian Fiction*

One may commence the first of the two interrelated acts of judgment—*Brave New World* as an artistic entity, as opposed to *Brave New World* as a diagnosis of the kind of world which Huxley and his contemporaries shared—by pointing to the esthetic problems which inhere in the writing of utopian fiction. Much modern fiction has the purpose of reflecting the reality which a writer shares with his readers. The starting-point of a realistic novel is the world as it is, whether the writer be a plodding realist like Arnold Bennett or a student of the deeper levels of experience that we call "psychological" (James Joyce or Virginia Woolf). The point of departure in such a novel is still the real world plus the sensibility of the artist who has written the novel. Sensibility, of course, leads to the transformations of reality that distinguish, for example, the novels of Virginia Woolf, from those of D. H. Lawrence; both writers shared a real world, and it is their various modes, of viewing reality that produce, in *Mrs. Dalloway* and in *Women in Love*, respectively, fictions that present "real" worlds drastically in contrast. Yet the supposition underlying judgment of these novels is that both *Mrs. Dalloway* and *Women in Love* tell about the world as it is.

With utopian fiction, the problem of achieving esthetic success becomes a much more complicated operation. The realistic novelist, psychological or otherwise, offers his world the flattering or unflattering mirror of his own sensibility. In a utopian novel another mirror is added; and the process by which reality is transformed is intensified. To the mirror of the writer's individual sensibility which reflects what reality is, there is added another which shows what reality might or should be. In consequence of the refraction and transformation of images, of reality, effected by this double mirroring, utopian fiction always offers to a given reality a complicated alteration. This alteration Huxley effected with full esthetic success only once; in *Brave New World*, the consciously distorted representation of certain current tendencies—faith in science, expectation that material and social progress will coincide—consistently reminds the reader of the real world that Huxley's mirrors are reflecting and yet speaks to the realization in the future of possibilities that are only stirring in the present. In much utopian fiction, the reality of the present, which writer and reader share, is frequently cheerfully sacrificed to the firm and tyrannical outlines of the utopian vision.

Huxley's two other utopian fictions—*Ape and Essence* (1948) and *Island* (1962)—are works that are esthetically unsatisfactory. *Ape and Essence* is inferior simply because of the superficiality with which the utopian task is performed; and *Island*, a more ambitious work, fails to please because the interplay of the "mirrors"—one for reality, one for the author's speculations about reality—does not really take place. Alternating in *Island* are techniques proper not only to representing a real, present world but to conveying utopian vision. In *Island* the world as it is and as it can be are both present but are discontinuously represented; the result is something like the layers of Neapolitan ice cream. In contrast, successful utopian fiction—and *Brave New World* has its position here—manages to blend these two opposed ways of viewing the world. Such fiction creates the sense that these two worlds coexist—indeed, have become one.

A cursory recollection of other utopian fiction can call to mind more failures than successes, if the suggested standard, that of temporary fusion, is acceptable. The vision of the ideal country offered in Sir Thomas More's *Utopia* is a manipulated one and no more; reality, in the sense of a continuation or presence of the early sixteenth-century world hangs above the surface of More's imagined island like an irrelevant mist, and the "should be" or "may be" takes precedence over any "is." In such a utopia, the existing and inescapable nature of man and his reactions—the problems of real human interrelations—are no more than fantasms that uneasily haunt the delineation of the new and better customs of "nowhere." The conditions of life as one knows it—in More's instance, as sixteenth-century men knew it— stand in a non-relation to the conditions of life as it might well be.

Because of this sort of artistic failure, much utopian fiction seems to be the graveyard of abortive human hope. The forgotten utopias of Ignatius Donnelley and the remembered ones of Edward Bellamy and H. G. Wells are, in their various ways, splendid and touching visions. They are splendid because they offer so much; they are often touching because they record a considerable blindness to what, in strength and weakness, lies in man. The vision is great and may be admired; but the vision is negated, reduced to empty fantasy, by what theologians would call the "anthropology" which informs many a utopia. The novelist's view of man determines whether his book will be empty or cogent. Too many utopian novels have been written by persons who failed to take into account the mixture of dream, courage, incontinence, and folly that man has always been and probably always will remain. From More's *Utopia* through Wells' *Men Like Gods* and B. F. Skinner's *Walden Two*, a distressing limitation is apparent. These books depict confidently the "shape of things to come"; but they often offer the reader shadows of men rather than the complex human beings, charged with both hope and perversity, whom one knows from direct experience.

Thus, the difficult task of the writer of utopian fiction is to achieve a double faithfulness. He must be faithful to the kind of knowledge he has of his fellow men and to his vision of a future time. One cannot say that the novels of Wells and Skinner achieve this double faithfulness. In these books, precise knowledge of man seems to be sacrificed to hopes for mankind. Such a sacrifice does not take place in the novels of Orwell, C. S. Lewis, and Aldous Huxley—at least, the Huxley of *Brave New World*. All three writers cherish a view of man that sees him hampered by limitations that are an essential part of his nature. That this is a view of man which is correct, that these limitations cannot be removed at some future time, is subject to question; and it may turn out that the hopes of Wells and Skinner have a firmer basis than either Orwell or Huxley would concede. If so, it will appear that Huxley was involved in a faithfulness that was misjudged.

The fictions of Huxley and Orwell, indeed, have been called "anti-utopias" since both men take a dark, rather than a confident view of the future possibilities of man. But an "altar of hope" is absent from Orwell and Huxley, not just because they do not in fact hope very confidently but because it demands the cancellation of what man is, in cheerful deference to what man may be. Neither Orwell nor Huxley is willing to sacrifice hard-earned knowledge of what man is (reality) to some scheme, some manipulated vision of what society could well be if, charmingly, man consented to be different. Neither Orwell nor the Huxley of *Brave New World* supposes that man has the power to annihilate himself as he is and become a footnote to a system. Man must remain, whatever the utopian setting imagination provides, the mixed, striving, inconstant being that he declares, to the attentive mind of the writer, he is. The utopias of Orwell and Huxley record, therefore, a refusal to streamline whatever knowledge of man they have.

The result of this refusal—and here one narrows his interest to Huxley's refusal and its consequences—is an imagined world of very complicated texture. What man is—for Huxley, for his reader—does not hang over the *Brave New World* landscape like a miasmal mist that the strategies of a better society will soon dissipate. What man is—at least, to the extent that Huxley was able to determine—becomes inextricably merged with what man has become in the imagined future, in the year 632 of Our Ford. The result, in *Brave New World*, of this preservation—of Huxley's cynically sharp, basically cold estimate of the poor forked creature named man is a work of the imagination that convinces rather than arouses amiable and delusory hope. What Huxley asserted about man in his first four novels is true in its own way. What Huxley asserts in *Brave New World* continues to have the same degree of truth. >From this one circumstance comes the power of the novel to delight in a sadistic way, and to horrify; the projected world has been successfully fused with what is. Another novelist's view of what is—C. S. Lewis', for example—would result in a very different utopia.

II. *Brave New World*

Brave New World opens ominously: the reader is taken on a supervised visit to the factory where the unborn or yet "undecanted" citizens of the "brave new world" are in the process of being created—not viviparously, but on the conveyor belts that, in dim antiquity, once carried Ford cars from start to finish on an assembly line. Here the reader sees the creation of beings who will not be individuals but will cheerfully belong to each other. In the famous phrase of the novel: "Everyone belongs to everyone else."

This "belonging" is not in the obvious sexual sense alone, for each child has his prenatal development controlled by scientifically determined admixtures of chemical. (An ill-adjusted person named Bernard Marx has been, it is speculated by his happy friends, damaged by an excess of alcohol administered to his foetus.) After decanting—birth—each person undergoes a process of "conditioning" that makes him a willing consumer of the pleasures of sex and sport and a fearful avoider of the pleasures and tastes that separate men from each other. Particular unnatural tastes for beauty, such as a non-consuming delight in bright flowers, is conditioned out of existence. By a process analogous to the famous experiment of Pavlov, who trained dogs to salivate at the sound of a bell rather than at the "natural" presence of food, children learn to fear pleasures that have no function in a tightly planned world.

Genetic differences in this anti-utopia have been foreseen and dealt with fairly well. By the process of Bokanovsky "budding," not just twins and triplets but as many as ninety-six persons are created from one sperm and one ovum. Diversity of social function demands the existence of different classes—Alpha, Beta, Gamma, and so forth—but submission to the conditions of life proper to one's class is rendered painless by hypnopaedia or "sleep teaching." In consequence, each child grows up thinking that his genetic inheritance and social position are indeed ideal. Each person is incapable of resentment when be observes the lot of others: those who direct the society do not, of course, resent those who take their directions; and those who obey have only pity for their superiors who carry a burden of responsibility that they are free from.

Furthermore, each person is incapable of expressing opinions or judgments of his own since these are, in theory and indeed usually in practice, non-existent; verbal education only prolongs the conformity that already existed on the assembly line along which fetuses pass. As the director of the hatcheries explains to his attentive pupils, the suggestions which each child unconsciously receives create the adult he becomes. The process continues "Till at last the child's mind is the child's mind. And not the child's mind only. The adult's mind too—all his life long. The mind that judges and desires and decides—made up of these suggestions." The Director concludes triumphantly: "But all these suggestions are our suggestions!" Thus does Huxley face the reader with the problem which has apparently vanished from the imagined commonwealth itself: *Quis custodiet custodes?*—who watches the watchmen?

The materials Huxley draws on for fabricating the utopian element in his novel are clearly the commonplaces of progressive hopes for mankind. In the early twentieth century, religious decay had removed from the minds of many enlightened men any expectation of a last judgment or of some other kind of divine intrusion into human experience. If men were to be saved, if the human experiment were to be salvaged and rendered more significant than that of the dinosaur, man must cease looking for aid to some deity he had himself invented in his own image; man must look to himself or, if not to himself, to the superior members of his species. These—not deity—can be expected to shape the destiny of future generations. Such superior persons must decide what man should become and then—by conditioning, by the ruthless imposition of adjustment to the "right" kind of social structure—see that all men become what, in the minds of intelligent planners, they ought to be.

These assumptions, as Huxley's satiric verve constantly suggests, are framed in a context of materialist convictions about what man is. Man is but a complex arrangement of chemical elements, and his proper satisfactions lie in the consumption of other chemical elements: material pleasures, physical actions that consume his tissues and necessitate the further intake of material items. Thus, in the novel, man passes his leisure hours in the execution of complex games like Centrifugal Bumble Puppy and Obstacle Golf; indulges in open and honest sexuality; or flies, if he is a member of the privileged classes, to any spot on earth in pursuit of amusement—which turns out to be much the amusement he has left behind. Thanks to social engineering, no one will be in want; and no one will, in consequence, have any cause to dream of other possible worlds. All men will have arrived at a point, itself a utopian one, where they will have no reason to have utopian dreams. And man's own nature, what we incorrectly call his "natural" discontents, will have been superseded by the comforts and certainties that exist under the sign of the Model T.

Huxley's ironical vision differs from two other notable ones of our time, E. M. Forster's *The Machine Stops* and Orwell's *Nineteen Eighty-Four*, in this respect: Huxley's utopia is assumed to be one which does its work well; but Forster and Orwell project visions of a future that does not live up to the scientific hopes which had created it. The irony that lies in the depiction of hopes that have been frustrated (as in Forster and Orwell) is indeed one that is easy to grasp. Huxley, instead, wishes to underline the irony inherent in the absolute success of a scientific-sociological vision.

This particular irony gives the reader the impact of what he and Huxley know man "is" on what (as the architects of the "brave new world" have seen the matter) man should be. Man, as Huxley views him in 1932, is not merely a creature capable of peace, harmony, and perfection under proper conditions; he is a creature, marked by confusion, fear, and deathlessly individual awareness. Did Huxley himself conceive man otherwise, the capacities and limitations of man in 1932 would be no more than the irritating mist that hangs at the horizon of much other utopian vision. But what man is in 1932 is a persisting element in what man has become in After Ford 632.

Future man, in Huxley's view, will be dogged by limiting insights that are at odds with the optimistic expectations of Sir Mustafa Mond and other planners. Future man will continue to be a creature who knows that he must die; and no supervised visits of the young to the state crematoria will really dissipate man's sense of his own contingency. No amount of neo-Malthusian drill in the schools will annihilate—at least in a few deviates like Bernard Marx and John, the Savage of the novel—the possibility that man is a creature who, sexually, can choose to exist for a particular other person rather than for everyone.

Bernard Marx, for example, looks at the calm yet rapturous face of a temporary sexual partner; "... the sigh of her transfigured face was at once an accusation and an ironical reminder of his own separateness." Nor will the pregnancy substitutes available to women turn out to be entirely satisfactory surrogates for the old, obscene experience of giving birth to children. Visits to the "feelies"—the improved "talkies" of A.F. 632—will not give the same results as emotion experienced and inspected in the separate human heart or soul. And it is doubtful that a drug named "soma" will do more than alleviate tensions endemic to man; it certainly will not cancel them. (Huxley is much indebted to the ancient Hindus in his later work; the borrowed term "soma" is an example of this debt.)

Huxley invents a story that makes these points aptly. After the opening visits to the assembly line that put in place the conditioned glories and securities of the imagined world, Huxley sends through their paces four or five main characters. These well-adjusted persons have such names as Lenina Crowne and, Helmholtz Watson (Huxley's malice appears in the invention of names which hark back to the chief cultural heroes of the nineteenth and twentieth centuries). There is the shrewd ruler of the "one world," Sir Mustafa Mond. There is the complacent director of the hatcheries. Less happy than these persons is Bernard Marx, perhaps damaged, as has been noted, by an excess of alcohol surrogate at an early stage in his physical development.

Indeed, the behavior of Bernard, stunted in height and hardly a worthy Alpha, is the first crack in the Eden of the future. Bernard yearns for nothing less than a permanent sexual relation with Lenina—a desire that strikes this modest girl as hardly decent. Pursuing his hope, Bernard persuades Lenina to go with him on a visit to an Indian reservation. There they encounter the Savage, John, in whom, finally, center all the disruptive elements of this future world—accurately reflecting Huxley's considered estimate of what man inescapably is.

The Savage—Huxley tells us—is the offspring of a "civilized" woman, who many years before had become lost in the Indian reservation; the father of the Savage, as it turns out, is the director of the hatcheries. The mother has shocked both the Indians and her son by her attempts to remain "decently" promiscuous in the uncivilized setting. Over the years, the Savage has learned to read Shakespeare; and in that corrupt author—otherwise known only to the director of civilized society, Sir Mustafa Mond—the young man has discovered models of behavior and feeling that had been edited out of the minds of the conditioned inhabitants of London and elsewhere.

As the Controller, Sir Mustafa Mond, explains, the reading of Shakespeare is dangerous. "Because it's old; that's the chief reason. We haven't any use for old things here." There is no room for tragedy or even for a desire to create works that reflect the vision that had overtaken the Savage in his adolescence—the interplay of life and time and death. In Mond's judgment, tragedy does not arise from man's situation; it once arose from the instability of a particular situation—one that in the new society has been erased: "The world's stable now. People are happy; they get what they want, and they never want what they can't get. They're well off; they're safe;

they're never ill; they're not afraid of death; they're blissfully ignorant of passion and old age; they're plagued with no mothers or fathers; they've got no wives, or children, or lovers to feel strongly about; they're so conditioned that they practically can't help behaving as they ought to behave. And if anything should go wrong, there's *soma*." This environment is disturbing chiefly to the rare Bernard Marxes of the happy society—and is doubly so to the Savage, who has escaped all the conditioning that makes the manipulated world a second Eden.

When the Savage is taken back to London as a curiosity, he shocks everyone by kneeling to his father, the director of the hatcheries. Shock and incomprehension become more intense when the Savage refuses to have casual sexual relations with Lenina. Certainly, no one in the "brave new world" understands his grief at the death of his silly mother; indeed, when the Savage falls to his knees grief-stricken, he is guilty of grave indecency, and his sorrow imperils the "wholesome death-conditioning" of the children standing in the hospital ward. The horrified nurse fears what his sobs may suggest—"as though death were something terrible, as though any one mattered as much as all that!" At this point and others, the Savage is an enigma that challenges all the self-evident truths on which the superior society has been built. For that matter, how is the Savage to emerge from the predicament in which he finds himself?

As Huxley points out in an introduction to the novel written in 1946, he saw at the time of writing only two possibilities for the Savage: conformity to the world into which he had been introduced or retreat to his passionate, Shakespeare-sponsored, "uncivilized" ways. The novel actually terminates with the death of the Savage, who has indulged in a *penitente* kind of self-flagellation to curb his lustful desires for Lenina—whom he finally kills because she represents to him all that is evil and yet attractive in sexuality.

In his 1946 introduction, Huxley observes that later years revealed to him that a third possibility existed for the Savage. This possibility came to dominate Huxley's mind as the years passed: "Science and technology would be used as though like the Sabbath, they had been made for man, not ... as though man were to be adapted and enslaved to them." Even religion would have its place—the kind of religion, of course, that offers valuable supplements to Christianity if it does not cancel it: "Religion would be the conscious and intelligent pursuit of man's Final End, the unitive knowledge of the immanent Tao or Logos...." And, as to what would be the prevailing philosophy of life—one apparently justifiable in contrast to "system"— Huxley answers: "... a kind of Higher Utilitarianism, in which the Greatest Happiness principle would be secondary to the Final End principle...." Had

Brave New World indeed embodied these possibilities, it would have (in Huxley's later judgment) possessed "artistic and a philosophic completeness, which in its present form it evidently lacks." It is more than incidentally significant that artistic and philosophic completeness are much the same thing and rest on the justice of the ideas expressed rather than on the problems of execution and form that usually go under the heading of "artistic."

At any rate, the Savage could have gone "beyond" or "above" both the conditioned security of London and the simplicities of the Indian reservation. He could have journeyed toward the insights into human capacity which Huxley, as a matter of fact, had not perceived with binding conviction at the time of writing *Brave New World*. But Huxley was, in the early 1930's, a "different person"; and, as biographical fact suggests, he was still somewhat influenced by the example of the last D. H. Lawrence, who had advocated a kind of visceral primitivism as the proper counter-irritant to a technologized civilization. The Huxley of 1946 had already said goodbye to D. H. Lawrence and to his kind of gospel in *Beyond the Mexique Bay* (1934), but be did not make any effort to adjust his 1932 account of human possibilities to later insight. *That* explicit effort appears in later utopian and non-utopian novels.

Indeed, one may fancy that *Brave New World* might have collapsed under the burden of the "Perennial Philosophy" which had taken command of Huxley's mind by 1946. The effective tension of *Brave New World* vibrates between the two clearly contrasting poles represented by London and the Indian reservation: the London, an achieved utopian future; the reservation, a confused museum of the past. Huxley tried, in his last novel, *Island*, to show man as struggling to go "beyond" the insights of 1932. This novel, with its more complex utopian problem, is an esthetic failure which is perhaps a reason for being content with the fact that the London of *Brave New World* is scanned, and rejected by a fairly simple set of standards.

III. *Esthetic Impact*

The esthetic success of *Brave New World* has already been suggested, but it should be underlined by reference to Huxley's earlier work. There are none of the false moves indicative of uncertainty of intent that mar a novel like *Those Barren Leaves*. The opening section in the hatchery employs the device of ironic counterpoint that was also successful in *Point Counter Point*. The mode of farce, so excellent in large sections of *Antic Hay*, finds a proper place in the depiction of the utopian world which Huxley has invented as a parody and intensification of all that is deleterious and threatening to human dignity in modern optimistic speculation. The "feelies," soma, conditioning—with terrific verve Huxley pushes these to their absurd logical extension. There is ample room—in this particular utopian vision—for the "savage indignation" that Huxley may have learned from Swift; for *Brave New World* is Huxley's counterpart of Swift's "modest proposal." The references to sexual drill and modish contraceptive belts are no more out of place than Swift's chilling suggestions about eating Irish children.

In abeyance—and happily, from artistic points of view—is the tragedy of solipsism that is seriously at odds with sheer satiric verve in all the earlier novels but *Crome Yellow*. Bernard Marx is doubtless potentially another solipsist, like Philip Quarles in *Point Counter Point*, and so in his way is the Savage. But the experiences of Bernard and the Savage remain assimilable parts of the general demonstration; they do not flaw the structure of *Brave New World* but intensify it by reminding the reader of what is being deformed and canceled by the efforts of directors like Sir Mustafa Mond.

Nor is there any manifestation of Huxley's tendency in later years to deviate into essay, to sacrifice the novel he is writing to cultural, political, and religious insight. In *Brave New World*, as some critics would say, the object is "rendered" rather than discussed. What discussion takes place occurs in the readers' minds and not in pages that would suspend the onrush of the nightmare that is, within its limits and in a very sinister way, absolutely true.

IV. *Symptomatic Implications*

One can have admiration for *Brave New World* as a work of art, but estimate cannot, of course, be limited to the esthetic success just looked at. *Brave New World* was also a work that expresses the twentieth-century cultural situation, as it has been known and experienced within the limits of Anglo-Saxon societies—and perhaps elsewhere. *Brave New World*, like much other work by Huxley, presupposes a certain set of expectations rejected and others reshaped or invented. It may indeed be regarded as a violent defense of and lament for the lapsed dignities of all mankind under threat of scientific encroachment. But it is more modest and more accurate to suggest that the novel is best read as a lament for the lapsed dignities of Protestant man.

These dignities were, as was noted in the second chapter of this book, questioned by the theories of Darwin and by debates about man's relation to God and the moral insights that were supposed to rest on this relation. These movements also had their impact elsewhere, but Anglo-Saxon man was peculiarly defenseless once the biblical sanction of morality and social structure was taken away. Once this was subtracted, what was left? In other cultures in the West, there were structures of church and state, even of sheer rationality and trust in it, that would sustain man. Elsewhere all coherence was not necessarily gone if, in Donne's phrase, the possibility of a confrontation between individual man and his God or (more modestly) individual man and his dignity were put in question.

The alternative to an evil world—in this novel, the Savage's flagellation and death—turns out to be, in Huxley's entire development, only a temporary one. In Huxley's later work, other figures take shape and, directed by the hand of the creator, sketch gestures and assume poses that leave behind the Savage and the book he finally dominates. But as a particular deposit of insight, the novel remains significant and continues to speak to later readers of what it is like to have lost one set of insights and to seek others—seek without taking up solutions offered by facile optimism. Huxley's own search did not, as noted already, conclude with *Brave New World*; it continues in the works now to be inspected.

JEROME MECKIER

Utopian Counterpoint and the Compensatory Dream

Counterpoint, as a technical and structural device within a particular novel, virtually disappears from Huxley's fiction after *Point Counter Point* and *Eyeless in Gaza*. But his three utopias—*Brave New World* (1932), *Ape and Essence* (1949), and *Island* (1962)—can best be examined as a series of intentional variations on the same themes: in short, as utopian counterpoint. Just as Huxley's first three novels form a natural trilogy each member of which deals with the same concerns in different ways, his three utopias, though scattered over a thirty-year period, are really part of one life-long endeavour. They offer three different presentiments of the future.

Ape and Essence, the novel that stands between the two more important utopias, is Huxley's version of the sort of twenty-second century that will result from a neglect of contemporary problems. Even the novel's arch-villain, the Arch-Vicar, is aware that the society over which he presides missed its great opportunity to evolve satisfactorily. Although *Brave New World* is also clearly the product of a continuation of trends Huxley saw with alarm in the 30s, the novel deals primarily with a civilization that has faced up to what Huxley considers the problems of the modern world but it has done so by answering all the right questions wrongly. By contrast, in *Island*, the Vedantist's utopia, Huxley offers his own version of the future. The Palanese have not missed the opportunity the society of *Ape and Essence*

From *Aldous Huxley: Satire and Structure.* © 1969 by Jerome Meckier.

neglected nor have they settled for the erroneous responses of Mustapha Mond and his fellow World Controllers.

By outlining two different ways of going forward in *Brave New World* and *Island*, and warning against one method of going backward in *Ape and Essence*, Huxley fulfils Quarles' prescription for the good novelist: 'A novelist modulates by reduplicating situations and characters' (XXII). *Brave New World* was conceived as a single work, but Huxley, as he added a second and then a third glance into the future, may have begun to see all three novels as part of one larger volume or concern. He created the second two as different aspects of the first. In *Ape and Essence*, he remedied an oversight he himself detected in *Brave New World*; and in *Island*, having found his own answers to the problems posed by the future, he rewrote *Brave New World* almost point by point. As in *Point Counter Point*, Huxley's goal, like that of Quarles, is 'Multiplicity of eyes and multiplicity of aspects seen' (XIV). He views the future first scientifically, in *Brave New World*, then as a combination of social planner and Vedantic philosopher in *Island*. By writing both positive and negative utopias, he attempts to dramatize in concrete form the advantages of what his essays recommend and the consequences of any continuation of the tendencies they satirize.

I

That Huxley should have written even one utopia is, from one point of view, very surprising. His early novels often seemed concerned mainly with exploding outworn ideas and revealing the mutual contradictoriness of modern alternatives. Readers of *Brave New World* invariably point to Mr. Scogan's comments in *Crome Yellow* as an indication of Huxley's perennial concern with the future. Indeed, Scogan, a gritty rationalist, could sue the author of *Brave New World*, for it contains little that he did not foresee. Scogan may, in fact, be a caricature of H. G. Wells, and it is thus intentionally ironic that his view of the future contrasts with his prehistoric appearance as a bird-lizard with an incisive beaked nose, dry and scaly skin, and the hands of a crocodile (III). Scogan predicts that, in the future, population will be obtained and controlled through bottle-breeding and the use of incubators. The family system, he continues, 'will disappear' (V) and Eros will be pursued without fear of consequences. At times he waxes lyrical over the prospect of 'the Rational State' wherein each child, properly classified by mind and temperament, will be duly 'labelled and docketed' for the education that will best enable him and his species 'to perform those functions which human beings of his variety are capable of performing'

(XXII). Even the one prediction Scogan is less specific about is relevant. He complains that 'For us', virtual prisoners of society and its impositions, 'a complete holiday is out of the question' (XXV). He may not envision soma itself, but he is aware of his Rational State's need for it.

However, despite what Scogan says in his capacity as a twentieth-century extension of the nineteenth-century progress-oriented reformer, Huxley's early prose is full of utopian disclaimers in which he greets the idea of writing a utopia with contempt. In one of his earliest remarks about utopian writers, Huxley condemns them, as he condemns most of his own characters, for escapism and eccentricity, for an egoistic inability to accept reality as they find it: 'Outward reality disgusts them; the compensatory dream is the universe in which they live. The subject of their meditations is not man, but a monster of rationality and virtue—of one kind of rationality and virtue at that, their own.' *Brave New World* is a 'monster of rationality' in which the rational is raised to an irrational power until, for example, the goal of sanitation reform in the nineteenth century, namely cleanliness, replaces godliness. Unfortunately, Huxley's comment about monsters of rationality also applies, eventually, to his own *Island*.

What Huxley's anti-utopian remarks in the late 1920s boil down to, then, is a hatred of the utopian speculations he was reading, or had read by 1930. Most of these, taking their cue from H. G. Wells, and ultimately from Bacon's *New Atlantis* (1627), were scientific. Those who foresee a utopian future, Huxley wrote, 'invoke not the god from the machine, but the machine itself'. Huxley's spoofing of the Wellsian notion that people in utopia should take turns doing high-brow and low-brow tasks: 'While Jones plays the piano, Smith spreads the manure' was just a preliminary for the full-fledged satire of *Brave New World*.

Thus although in one sense Huxley's novels and non-fiction prose prior to 1932 seemed to indicate that he would never stoop to utopian themes, in another they made *Brave New World* inevitable. One of the chief reasons why Huxley wrote the novel, it is tempting to conclude, was to discredit, if not discourage, the sort of utopian writing he was familiar with. The urge to write a literary satire on existing works went hand in hand with the desire to challenge, by means of a correcting, less optimistic vision of his own, the picture of the future that science was enthusiastically offering. In his prose essays, Huxley 'was thus composing *Brave New World* for years before starting the novel itself. In essays from *Music at Night*, such as 'Liberty and the Promised Land', 'History and the Past', 'Wanted a New Pleasure', and throughout *Proper Studies*, Huxley was indulging in distopian prose, from which the anti-utopian or distopian novel and eventually the positive utopia spring almost inevitably. The difference between the satirist and the writer of utopias is somewhat minimal to begin with, since the second, like the first, intends to expose the difference between what he beholds and what he would prefer to see. Once the anti-utopian novel is written, its counterpart already exists by implication. As Huxley became increasingly convinced that he had found the true path, he employed the medium of a positive utopia to explore a future of his own conceiving. Eventually, Huxley, too, disclosed his compensatory dream.

Even the anti-utopian non-fiction prose just mentioned, however, is hardly free of moments when Huxley is possibly not ridiculing scientific utopias, when he seems, instead, intrigued by their possibility—an attitude which often makes the reader suspect that *Brave New World* is not the total satire some critics claim. The question of 'eugenic reform' always has a fascination for Huxley. He entertains it in *Music at Night* as a means of raising the critical point beyond which increases in prosperity, leisure, and education now give diminishing returns. He even speaks, with apparent tolerance, of a new caste system based on differences in native ability and of an educational process that supplies an individual with just so much instruction as his position calls for. He worries, in *Proper Studies*, about the threat to the world's IQ that the more rapidly reproducing inferior classes constitute. And when, in an essay catalogued above as distopian prose, he predicts that society 'will learn to breed babies in bottles', or talks, albeit somewhat critically, of theatres wherein 'egalitarians' will enjoy talkies, tasties, smellies, and feelies, he almost seems to become Scogan.

Huxley is even more eloquent than Scogan on the possibilities of a holiday-inducing drug when he writes that: 'If we could sniff or swallow something that would, for five or six hours each day, abolish our solitude as individuals ... earth would become paradise.' What Scogan wanted was an escape hatch, but what Huxley wants is a means of breaking down the individual's isolation within his own ego. The difference between the two positions, however, is not so clear as to make pointing it out unnecessary. The drug called soma in *Brave New World* is not inherently unsatisfactory, but rather is an inadequate surrogate for something Huxley would accept in a more proper form.

And yet *Brave New World* is not utopia but distopia, even if the problems its society has confronted are the same ones the Palanese of *Island* must face. The difference between *Island* and *Brave New World* is that the Palanese have correctly solved the problems Mustapha Mond and his fellow World Controllers have mismanaged. This will become clearer subsequently in a discussion of the ways in which *Island* is Huxley's corrective for *Brave*

New World. What has escaped notice and what is possibly the surest way of discrediting the society of *Brave New World* is the fact that, judged on its own terms, it is manifestly a failure. All the old problems exist in new forms and the new society's use of language is one long and recurrent illustration of how life has not gained in meaning but become instead absolutely meaningless.

To begin with, despite the complicated mechanical processes at work in *Brave New World*, the manner in which each individual is artificially born on a sort of Fordian assembly line and trained for one job only, human errors persist. These are not only still made, but take infinitely longer to be discovered. Lenina, musing about the Savage, who has only recently arrived from a reservation outside the brave new world, forgets to give a bottle-baby its sleeping sickness injection and twenty-two years later an Alpha-Plus administrator becomes the first trypanosomiasis fatality in over half a century (XIII). Though it requires nearly a quarter of a century to happen, people still die from birth defects. Similarly, Bernard Marx's eccentric love of solitude and his fondness for walks in the Lake District are attributed to an overdose of 'Alcohol in his blood-surrogate' (VI). One might add that all babies born in *Brave New World* have what Huxley would consider birth defects: each is conditioned to do the same task over and over again and is thus as one-pointed or one-sided from birth as any typical eccentric in the four Huxley novels that precede *Brave New World*.

The problem of mental–physical imbalance has not been completely solved either. It exists in *Brave New World* just as it did for the imbalanced heroes of Huxley's previous novels. The ideal of proportion, a state of body–mind equilibrium recommended throughout *Antic Hay*, is still unattained: 'A mental excess had produced in Helmholtz Watson effects very similar to those which, in Bernard Marx, were the result of a physical defect' (IV). Both men, the antihero, Bernard, and the slogan-writer, Helmholtz, are misfits in a society that claims to have found the proper place for everyone. When the Savage arrives, the number of misfits increases to three. Even Lenina, who in so many ways is the product of her upbringing and who proves as disillusioning an experience for Bernard and the Savage as Barbara was for Chelifer in *Those Barren Leaves*, is not perfectly conditioned. She asks Bernard at one point if he still desires to spend a week with her. He blushes and she is 'astonished' by such a response, 'but at the same time touched by this strange tribute to her power' (IV). Cracks in everyone's conditioning are woefully apparent. The Epsilon-Minus Semi-Moron who operates a lift is startled 'from a dark annihilating stupor' by the 'warm glory of afternoon sunlight' as his elevator reaches the roof of the Central London Hatchery (IV).

Despite the complete mechanization of the birth process and the acceleration achieved by the Bokanovsky Process coupled with Podsnap's technique, it still takes 267 days, or three days less than nine months, to produce a child (I). The Bombay Green Rocket may do 'Twelve hundred and fifty kilometres an hour', as the Station Master boasts it can, but it is no substitute for the human imagination. 'Ariel', the Savage points out, 'could put a girdle round the earth in forty minutes' (XI). Even the womb complex survives in a new and curious form. In the Westminster Abbey Cabaret, the Sexophonists sing: 'Bottle of mine, it's you I've always wanted! / Bottle of mine, why was I ever decanted?' (V).

The society of *Brave New World* still resorts to escapism, just as the typical Huxley character always inhabits a self-enclosed private world of his own. By means of soma, one can now take a holiday from reality almost at will. Even within a society supposed to be the realization of the compensatory dream, a means for additional compensation must be maintained. Nor have the inadequacies of organized religion been eliminated. Instead, the tops are sawed off all crosses to make T's, and the masses make 'the sign of the T' on their stomachs, presumably in deference to Ford's model-T car and the scientific know-how that feeds them (II). The new is consistently similar, even inferior, to the old. Thus although old taboos have been destroyed, the same youths who say 'ovary' and 'sperm' without hesitation snigger at new artificial obscenities such as 'parent' or 'mother' (II). The twentieth-century may have foolishly banned *The Rainbow* and *Ulysses*, but Mond's world has its own peculiar 'pornography', namely *The Imitation of Christ* and *The Varieties of Religious Experience* (XVII).

The result in *Brave New World* of society's admiration for scientific advances and of its worship of progress—two attitudes Huxley cannot share—is a condition in which neither is any longer allowable. But the consequences of progress have produced something very similar to the sort of society that existed in the mid-nineteenth century. The best society, contends Mustapha Mond, is like the iceberg: eight-ninths below the water line and one-ninth above (XVI). What the people of *Brave New World* have accomplished by the most exacting scientific controls, the Victorians achieved through *laissez-faire*. Admittedly, the eight-ninths now below the water line are neither desperately poor nor thoroughly diseased, yet they can hardly be called conscious of their comfort. The class system has been replaced by something worse, namely a caste system with Alphas on top and moronic Epsilons at the bottom.

Formerly, Mustapha Mond claims, 'exclusiveness, a narrow channelling of impulse and energy' was everywhere the rule, but now 'every one belongs to every one else' (III). Unfortunately, Mond's statement, though cast in general and universal terms, has an exclusive, narrow meaning. It means that promiscuity is now possible for everyone. In terms of jobs, education, and emotional life, the 'narrow channelling' practised by *Brave New World* is unprecedented. Diversity has been completely eliminated and the individual, previously an unpredictable quantity, now remains 'Constant throughout a whole lifetime' (III). The one-pointedness for which Huxley always satirizes his egocentric characters is now built into them from birth.

Worst of all, language has virtually lost its meaning and few speakers in this model world of scientifically engineered precision realize how unscientific and imprecise their words really are. Many of the characters have Marxist names (Lenina, Bernard Marx, Polly Trotsky) and Benito Hoover's name is an oxymoronic combination of capitalism and Fascism, but none of them have any notion of Russian history or of what genuine Communism is. Helmholtz Watson's name, a curious amalgam of Hermann Ludwig von Helmholtz (1821–1894), the German scientist, and Sir William Watson (1858–1935), an English poet, seems to imply that science and art are now united, but innocuously so, in the job of furnishing slogans for the state. In fact, the famous names of these characters form a pointed contrast to a World State that is simply one of Henry Ford's Detroit plants magnified many times. Polish, French, and German are now classified among the dead languages (II), and that is also where the Savage's pure Shakespearian English belongs (VII), especially the allusion he (seriously) and the novel's title (ironically) make to Miranda's speech in *The Tempest* (V, i, 181–184).

What happens to the meaning of *normality* when Mr. Foster explains he wants to give the Epsilon embryo 'the normality of dogs and cows' (I)? Does Foster realize what he is saying when he remarks that on the morning of the 267th day, in the Decanting Room, the bottle baby achieves 'Independent existence—so called' (I)? The once powerful theological term 'predestination' now means little more than suiting people to an 'unescapable social destiny' (I). When Lenina describes her Malthusian belt, itself a preventive or substitution device, as 'real morocco-surrogate' (III), one realizes how confused the relation between things and words has become. Can individuals who have not blood but 'blood surrogate' in their veins be termed human at all? The fact that women must take a 'Pregnancy Substitute' (III) to satisfy maternal urges underlines the extent to which *Brave New World*, in words and objects, is a world of facsimiles behind which certain genuine human feelings faintly persist.

From chapter to chapter the destruction of the meaning of words proceeds apace. Foster explains that childhood has been abolished because the years between an Epsilon's birth and the time he is fit for work constitute a 'superfluous and wasted immaturity' (I). Yet the Epsilon's so-called maturity is scarcely that of a five-year-old. Surely this is no great improvement on the treatment of children in nineteenth-century England. It would be too painful to point out the real meaning of each word in 'Community, Identity, Stability', the motto of *Brave New World*. And the same holds true for *group* in the scientific term 'Bokanovsky Group'. How meaningless the Savage's condemnation of the promiscuous Lenina—'Whore!' he shouted. 'Whore! Impudent strumpet!' (XIII)—has become in a society where chastity is non-existent as a word or a concept.

In short, there is an overwhelming discrepancy between the reality of *Brave New World* and the picture it has formed of itself by means of its language. So much of the language used in *Brave New World* is not really stable, but is, like society and the formerly diverse individual, artificial, stagnant, virtually dead. Like the egoist-poet Denis in *Crome Yellow*, the society of *Brave New World* chooses words over things and makes an object an illustration of the word whether it is so or not.

In his 'Forward' (1947) to a re-printing of *Brave New World*, Huxley calls science 'Procrustes in modern dress' and laments the fact that mankind will be made to fit the bed science provides for it. Linguistically, this process is already far advanced. If the brave new world cannot insert a square peg into a round hole it will redefine roundness until a perfect fit results. Huxley is fully aware of the dangers inherent in any misuse of language, of the manifold ways in which a loss or perversion of the meaning of words furthers the designs of any centralized power, whether it is as inhumanly benevolent as Mustapha Mond or as blatantly militaristic as Col. Dipa of Rendang in *Island*. In *Words and Their Meanings* (1940), 'Words and Behaviour' in *The Olive Tree* (1937), and in *Brave New World Revisited* (1958), Huxley insists on the precise use of language as a safeguard against societies such as that of *Brave New World*. It comes as no surprise that the Palanese children of *Island* are given 'systematic and carefully graduated training in perception and the proper use of language' (XIII).

It is this awareness of the relation between the perversion of language and the rise of a centralized authority that possibly constitutes Huxley's main contribution to distopian literature. In George Orwell's *1984* (1949), O'Brien and his group, the Party, have at their disposal a whole new language (Newspeak). Eventually it will guarantee their stay in power. The eleventh edition of the Newspeak Dictionary will make thought contrary to the Party's purposes an impossibility. Even so marginal a utopian work as Anthony Burgess' *The Clockwork Orange* (1963) seems implicitly to realize that to control a person's life and thought one need only manipulate his language. (The crudeness, the monosyllabic quality of much of the language used by Burgess' characters, may be the key to their bestial conduct.) Thus Mustapha Mond confiscates the work of an author who, like Huxley, both debunks the ideal of happiness as a sovereign good and talks, like Mr. Propter, of a 'goal ... outside the present human sphere,' of an 'enlargement of knowledge' (XII). Thus Helmholtz Watson lacks the words and experiences for the serious literature he desires to write (XII).

Art, science, truth, and beauty may indeed be irreconcilable with comfort and happiness, as Mustapha Mona maintains (XVI), but one suspects this is because comfort and happiness have been assigned rather original meanings. Only in *Brave New World* could Mond argue that the religious sentiment is unnecessary because the population is death-conditioned and the concept of death has lost its meaning. The moral sense has been replaced by continued prosperity and sanctioned self-indulgence. Mond consciously typifies his society's linguistic practices when he explains to the Savage that God now 'manifests himself as an absence' (XVII).

II

Brave New World has much in common with the whole range of utopian literature, some of which Huxley appears to have had at his fingertips as he wrote. One is tempted to point out that utopian literature, like mysticism, is virtually a tradition in which an author can immerse himself and find innumerable guidelines, such as Samuel Butler's *Erewhon*, which Huxley edited in 1934. A good deal of the success of *Brave New World* and of the weakness of *Island* becomes clearer in light of the utopian tradition.

One of the ways in which Huxley's first utopia resembles its predecessors is in its use of a device that can be called the familiar–unfamiliar. The novel opens *in medias res* and showers the reader with a series of unexplained details. So much of the appeal of any utopian work depends on its initial sense of mystery and the reader's correspondent demand for an explanation. It is essential what exactly Alphas, Betas, Deltas, and Epsilons are. Central London sounds familiar enough, but the Central London Hatchery and Conditioning Centre (I) is at first an unknown quantity, an even more intriguing enigma than 'the famous British Museum massacre' (III). Huxley suddenly introduces the reader into a new world, and it is not until the momentum with which puzzling details are presented slows down that one becomes an informed visitor and is ready for an explanation of how the society one lives in has become the society one is reading about.

Frequently the new and puzzling items have a partially familiar aspect: Big Henry (V) or *The Fordian Science Monitor* (XVIII). Interest is thus generated by the presentation of things already known but seen now in new combinations or an unfamiliar light. In William Morris' *News From Nowhere* (1897), for example, the Houses of Parliament are still recognizable to Mr. Guest but their use as a storage place for manure is startling (V). The picture of post-World-War-III California, with its ghost town of Los Angeles, thrusts the reader of *Ape and Essence* into a world he feels he partially knows but is totally unaccustomed to seeing in this fashion.

Like most previous utopias, *Brave New World* does its share of prophesying. It makes predictions about the future, and, as a lengthy analysis of *Brave New World Revisited* would show, is often close to the mark. Its second sight in describing the future importance of drugs (a factor in the novel's continued popularity) is paralleled by the nonchalance with which it permits its characters to use a machine that has now become the familiar helicopter. The personages in Edward Bellamy's *Looking Backward* (1888) employ something very similar to the modern credit card (IX). And Bellamy's phrase 'from the cradle to the grave' (IX), as a summary of the extent to which his utopian government supervises its people's needs, clearly anticipates the Welfare State. As Professor Burris notes in XX of B. F. Skinner's *Walden Two* (1948), Samuel Butler in *Erewhon* (1872) 'accurately ... predicted the modern change in attitude toward criminal and moral lapses'. In *We* (1924), a distopia by the Russian, Eugene Zamiatin, that influenced Wells, Orwell, and Huxley, everyone has a number for a name and interplanetary rockets as well as much of modern Russia's political machinery are plausibly described.

Thus utopias are not only about the future but written for the future as well, either to represent a perennial and unattainable ideal or as a description of a state of affairs that is, for better or worse, to be realized gradually in succeeding years. When first read, they are both familiar and unfamiliar. With respect to some of their aspects one is in a totally new world, but other items are both old and new. However, it is the familiar that should increase—whether in the positive, practical utopia of Bellamy or the nightmarish distopia of Orwell—as the gap between the foreseen utopia and the actual world narrows. There are literally hundreds of utopias that are no longer readable, except as literary history, because little of what they envisioned ever came to pass. Part of the persuasiveness of any good positive utopia and much of the horror in any distopia stem from the reader's conviction that he already lives in the initial stages of the society the utopian author describes and that he may live to witness the complete identification of fiction and reality. The truly great utopias maintain this power to convince long after they are written, even if the predictions they make are not yet accomplished and may never be. Francis Bacon's vision of a world dominated by science has come true in numerous respects, though neither Huxley nor Orwell are pleased. Thomas More's *Utopia* is scarcely closer to realization today than it was in 1516, but the Europe he found fault with has not totally changed and certain facets of his ideal state still retain the power to excite the imagination.

Both More and Plato, the latter in his *Republic* (380–370 B.C.), seem to have been interested in exhibiting what they themselves saw as a probably permanent gap between the ideal society and those in which men would always live. More modern utopias, following Bacon rather than More, appear to be written in the belief they represent, for better or worse, the world of the author's grandchildren. This is certainly true of Bellamy, Wells, Huxley, and Orwell, though not perhaps of Butler. The difference between some sections of Bellamy or Orwell and a factual article by John R. Pierce about events almost imminent is often minimal.

Plato and More were classical even as they wrote. They were describing what they saw as a perennially ideal but unattainable state rather than offering a blueprint for the immediate or even distant future. More's *Utopia* and Bacon's *New Atlantis* were seen already existing in some unfrequented corner of the globe that was virtually synonymous with their creators' imaginations or with some vanished golden age. In Bacon, the ideal seems to be a combination of the unfallen past and a progressive future. Since Bacon, however, utopias seem to have become more and more practical until the golden age or its opposite is in the immediate future. In Orwell, the gap between composition and realization has narrowed from the century and a half of *Ape and Essence* to a mere thirty-five years, although what readers will make of *1984* in the years 1985 and following remains to be seen.

Unlike *Island*—in fact, unlike most of utopian literature in English with the exception of *1984*—*Brave New World*, and *Ape and Essence* to a lesser degree, do not have the almost inevitable breaking point where most of the novelty vanishes to be replaced by a tedious essay. Once Guest learns where he is and what century it is, the rest of Morris' book belongs to garrulous Old Hammond. In *Island*, after the initial strangeness of Pala wears off, the book becomes a series of essays spoken in the direction of Will Farnaby by a number of characters who know Huxley's views. Orwell does have to permit his hero, Winston, to read Goldstein's book so the reader will understand how the Party rose to power, but the book device is quite dissimilar from the rest of *1984*, whereas Will's conversations with the MacPhails and his perusal of *Notes on What's What* are almost identical. Although it is preoccupied with the perennial utopian concerns (centralization versus decentralization, reform of the family, experiments in breeding and in education), *Brave New World* escapes many of the traditional weaknesses of utopian writings. So too with *Ape and Essence*, even if it cannot match the former for its extravagant sense of humour and occasionally hyperbolic style. Both works contain a sufficiently interesting plot to keep them in motion after the novelty of their respective milieus begins to fade.

What *Brave New World* actually involves is a doubling of the device by which initial strangeness is usually secured. Throughout the opening chapters, it is the reader who plays the part of Morris' Mr. Guest or Bellamy's Mr. West. It is the reader who, like Swift's, Gulliver, has landed in a strange world. After ten chapters, the device is used all over again as the Savage from a New Mexican reservation lands in London. The reader must then compare his own reactions to the new world with John's. In addition, the introduction of a second visitor or stranger, the reader being the first, provides Huxley with the opportunity of using the Wellsian scientific future, represented by London, and the Lawrencian primitive past, as personified by the Savage, to discredit each other. This reaches its climax in the confrontation scene between John and Mustapha Mond in which both speakers' viewpoints are exposed as incomplete and the speakers themselves become parallel lines (XVII), like Denis and Mary in *Crome Yellow* (XXIV). The world Mond argues for is in need of the beauty poetry can provide, while John's world overlooks the advantages science offers.

The extent to which *Brave New World* satirizes previous utopias, particularly the Wellsian utopia, demands an essay in itself. There is a sense in which Wells exhibits the nineteenth century in what he considers its ultimate and ideal form while Huxley presents the same century and its goals (controlled evolution, happiness) carried to an alarmingly successful and essentially insane conclusion. Wells' Samurai from *A Modern Utopia* (1905) become Huxley's World Controllers. Wells' prediction of the increased role of the machine, his concern with controlled breeding, his classification of inhabitants by temperament and mental ability—all of these are satirized in Huxley's distopia. In fact, Wells' *The First Men in the Moon* (1901) may be the chief target and inspiration behind *Brave New World*. The Selenite community of ant-like creatures Bedford and Cavor stumble on and that Cavor describes at length (XXIII–XXIV) is virtually identical with the London Huxley creates in *Brave New World*, except that Cavor is ambiguously pro and con in his reactions to the Selenites in a way that Huxley, in satirizing Wells, chooses to ignore.

Largely because it is a distopia aimed at discrediting the utopian musings of Wells and Lawrence, *Brave New World* escapes the 'pervading smugness of tone' that Northrop Frye correctly finds in most self-satisfied utopian planners, and that he would no doubt detect in *Island*. If one reads a speech of Morris' Old Hammond (or of Bellamy's Dr. Leete) along with one from Huxley's Dr. MacPhail, all three spokesmen turn out to be certain they live in the best of possible worlds, but all three cannot be correct. Most positive utopias fail to prove, though most assume, that a changed social environment means better people. One generally feels, however, that the writer is incredibly naive, that it was human nature that miraculously changed first and society afterwards. Neither Morris, Bellamy, nor the Huxley of *Island* can convince one differently.

Despite supposedly humanistic aims, the utopian author often appears to have insurmountable prejudices. His utopia permits him to assume the privileges of a god and recreate the world in his own image. Morris' prejudices are writ large in *News From Nowhere*, in which the perfect society is his own medieval dream come true and everyone is transformed into a practising craftsman. By turning his own workshop into the pattern for an entire world, Morris personifies the egotism and wish-fulfilment inherent in most positive utopian conceptions, Huxley's *Island* of mystics included.

The gravest weakness of almost all utopias, however, is their unattractiveness as possible places to live. Few are open-ended enough to allow for additional change. Bellamy's seems so perfect yet so dull. Morris' is terribly provincial and incurious. Wells' *A Modern Utopia* (1905) insists there is 'no limit to the invasion of life by the machine', but his ideal society, like Plato's, has an oppressive air of assured stability. It is this stagnant quality that Mustapha Mond's society represents at its worst and that O'Brien's Party in *1984*, by different means, is trying to achieve. Of all the positive utopias written over the past century, *Island* is one of the few in which life preserves some variety and excitement. How to be stable without becoming stagnant is a problem no positive utopia has ever perfectly solved. Much of the excitement in *Island* may in fact be due simply to Pala's tenuous existence as an ideal spot in an otherwise non-utopian world.

What this brief and by no means inclusive section on Huxley in relation to other utopians has tried to suggest is that Huxley was aware of his place in a long line of utopian writers. He borrowed from, openly imitated, and at times severely satirized his predecessors. Also, his distopias, because they are by nature negative and because they are seriously concerned with plot, avoid the failings common to most positive utopias, including Huxley's own *Island*. The distopia appears to be the generically superior literary form. That Huxley eventually attempted the positive form of utopian composition, a form in which the weaknesses catalogued above are virtually inherent, is a tribute more to the strength of his convictions than to his literary sagacity. Nevertheless, the positive utopia catered to the ever-present essayist in Huxley. It was the logical outcome for a novelist concerned with ideas but who became, from *Eyeless in Gaza* onwards, less interested in dramatizing or personifying them. The world we are creating, Orwell writes in *1984*, 'is the exact opposite of the stupid hedonistic Utopias that the old reformers imagined'. But once this new sort of world is exposed, the allure of the positive utopias of the past, for Huxley if not for Orwell, becomes harder to resist.

III

Though one reviewer called *Ape and Essence* a 'merciless allegory', Huxley saw it as a partial redressing of a cruel oversight in *Brave New World*. In his 1947 'Forward' to *Brave New World*, Huxley complained that the Savage retreats into despair because he is given a choice between two undesirables: an insane modern utopia and an unappetizing reservation life. Huxley has either forgotten, or chooses to disregard, the isolated community to which Helmholtz Watson and Bernard Marx are deported. It is, however, under Mustapha Monds jurisdiction and the Savage would never have been offered the chance to go there. 'If I were now to rewrite the book,' Huxley said in 1947, 'I would offer the Savage a third alternative. Between the utopian and the primitive horns of his dilemma would lie the possibility of sanity—a possibility already actualized, to some extent, in a community of exiles and refugees from the Brave New World, living within the borders of the Reservation.' This community, with its decentralized economics and sane use of science, would be primarily concerned with 'man's Final End'. Huxley is describing what he will eventually develop into the Pala of *Island*. But he also has in mind, in 1947, the community of 'Hots' Alfred Poole and Loola flee to at the end of *Ape and Essence* (1949), a novel that includes the all-important trap door of justifiable escape.

To understand *Ape and Essence* thoroughly and pinpoint its role in Huxley's utopian trilogy, one must first grasp Huxley's idea of commendable evolution as described by both Mr. Propter in *After Many a Summer Dies the Swan* and Sebastian Barnack in *Time Must Have a Stop*. Pete Boone asks: 'Where ought we to fight for good?' And Propter replies: 'On the level below the human and on the level above. On the animal level and on the level ... of eternity' (Part 1, IX). It is the middle plateau of time, personality, and craving that is irredeemably evil. Sebastian offers an additional explanation. In the 'Epilogue' (XXX), he defines life as a progression 'from animal eternity into time, into the strictly human world of memory and anticipation; and from time, if one chooses to go on, into the world of spiritual eternity, into the Divine Ground.' *Brave New World* and *Island* chronicle the attempts of two different societies to progress from the world of time, memory, and anticipation. Where *Island* seeks 'the world of spiritual eternity', *Brave New World* dwells in the eternal now of a life-style that has abolished the past (memory) and ignores the future (anticipation). History, in the words of Our Ford, is bunk (III). 'Was and will make me ill, I take a gramme and only am,' Lenina recites (VI).

By contrast with his other two utopias, *Ape and Essence* is a story of retrogression and recovery. In it Huxley reconsiders his predictions for the future so as to allow for the possibility of a devastating war and a reversion to 'animal eternity'. Where *Brave New World* and *Island* deal with steps forward, *Ape and Essence* is thus a step backward. Like the Fifth Earl of Hauberk in *After Many a Summer Dies the Swan*, the inhabitants of post-World-War-III America have fallen from the world of time to become more simian than human. As Propter would have realized, if men descend to the animal level, they must regain the human before attempting to climb onto the level of eternity. Dr. Alfred Poole and the simple-minded Loola become the potential Adam and Eve of a new race once they escape from the ape-like society of twenty-second-century California to go in search of a more complete way of life. Because they fall truly in love, Alfred and Loola can live on the 'animal level' in a different and more promising way than those they flee from. What they discover on this 'animal' or physical level awakens Poole to the higher possibilities. It is on the animal level that he begins to fight for good.

Ape and Essence is written from a sort of historical viewpoint. In one sequence Huxley presents the New Zealand Rediscovery Expedition landing on what it believes to be a totally uninhabited America. It is February 20, 2108. New Zealanders have not travelled anywhere for over a century due to the radioactive condition of the rest of the world. This puts the destruction one may call World War III in the late twentieth or early twenty-first century. Because of its geographic isolation, New Zealand is the only country that survived the war intact. In a second sequence, Huxley flashes back to battle scenes from World War III and to the meretricious culture of a pre-war America the reader is supposed to recognize as the present. These two sequences are handled in alternating sections which unfortunately fail as effective counterpoint, The World War III scenes seem too heavily satiric and allegoric ('Church and State / Greed and Hate! / Two Baboon Persons in One Supreme Gorilla'), while the frequent images of 'an almost unruffled sea' and an imperturbable blue sky are blatant symbols of an ignored timelessness or eternity. Ostensibly, *Ape and Essence* pretends to be a film script by a certain William Tallis. Huxley stumbles on the script by accident (it falls off a truck taking papers to the incinerator) and he prints it 'as I found it'. But the core of the novel depends on a comparison of the way the world was destroyed with the way it is being re-discovered.

These two alternating processes are depressingly similar. For one thing, the old America was destroyed by science and is being rediscovered by scientists. Dr. Poole's nickname, 'Stagnant', thus seems to stand not only for his lacklustre emotional life but also for science's contribution to a historical process that is cyclical rather than progressive. The battlefield scenes from World War III show two armies of baboons engaged in combat, each army with a captive Einstein on a leash. The two Einsteins are the last to die and the Narrator, whose voice breaks into the script at frequent intervals, pronounces 'the death by suicide of twentieth-century science'. When Dr. Poole of the Rediscovery Expedition is captured by the race of baboon-like humans who survived the holocaust in America, their chief is overjoyed. He asks Poole if New Zealand has trains, engines, and modern scientific conveniences. When Poole replies affirmatively, the Chief exclaims: 'Then you can help us to get it all going again.' Even Poole's objection that he is only a biologist who studies plant life fails to dampen the Chief's enthusiasm. 'War plants?' he asks hopefully.

After Poole is forcibly conducted to this primitive society's main base, the device of the familiar–unfamiliar takes over. Los Angeles has become a ghost town, and the main occupation of the surviving Americans is scavenging in graveyards for clothes there are no longer any factories to produce. Books are transported from the nearby Public Library to provide fuel for bakery ovens.

From the Arch-Vicar, a high-ranking member of the society's eunuch priesthood, Poole learns that the causes of World War III were all the things the reader will remember Huxley castigating in his essays of the 1930s and 40s. *Ape and Essence*, though written later, is less futuristic than *Brave New World* and more Orwellian. Throughout *Ape and Essence*, Huxley operates from the premise that an Orwellian vision of the future may be more reliable than his own, and he tries to envision what will happen to his own positive concerns in an Orwellian world. Before Mustapha Mond's society came into being, struggles such as the 'famous British Museum massacre' took place. Pre-war America was in a similarly restive state, only the war that followed there had more destructive consequences. Huxley realizes that overpopulation, for example, may lead to World War III before it will occasion controlled breeding, although it may eventually cause the latter also. Before World War III, as *Ape and Essence* makes clear, there were in fact too many people for too little food.

Also responsible for World War III were the false utopian ideals represented by Progress (the theory that utopia lies ahead and ideal ends justify abominable means) and Nationalism (the theory that the state one lives in is utopia and the only true deity). Here the echoes of essays in *An Encyclopedia of Pacifism* and in *Ends and Means* are unmistakable. 'As I read history,' says the Arch-Vicar, 'it's like this. Man putting himself against Nature, the Ego against the Order of Things. Belial ... against the Other One.' Thus egotism, Huxley's perennial enemy, also played a significant part. In fact, the ego has been objectified by the surviving Americans as the Devil himself and worshipped accordingly. The priests wear horns instead of mitres and 'May you never be impaled on His Horns' becomes a form of well-wishing.

Undercutting the simian antics of all Poole meets are the Narrator's recurring lines: 'But man, proud man, / Drest in a little brief authority—/ Most ignorant of what he is most assured. His glassy essence—like an angry ape, / Plays such fantastic tricks before high heaven / As make the angels weep.' The lines, originally spoken by Isabella in *Measure for Measure* (II, ii, 117–122), clearly emphasize the choices as retrogression or devolution as opposed to recognition in man of an inherent spiritual principle ('glassy essence'), which Sebastian Barnack of *Time Must Have a Stop* would call the Atman.

Nowhere does the choice the society of *Ape and Essence* has made become so evident as in the yearly ritual that includes Belial Eve and Belial Day. These occasions comprise the annual mating season, a brief orgiastic respite from an otherwise total sexual repression. Where *Brave New World* sanctioned promiscuity, *Ape and Essence* enforces continence for most of the year. All women conceive at about the same time and most children are born during one period some nine months later. Purification Day, on which all babies born with deformities due to radioactivity are systematically destroyed, is made possible by a controlled breeding period not unlike what Plato recommends in his *Republic* (v) and by the almost simultaneous births that result. For the Belial Day ceremonies, the women discard the 'NO' patches sewn onto their breasts and buttocks. In effect, humans now have the same breeding habits as animals, 'sex has become seasonal', and, as the Narrator remarks, the 'female's chemical compulsion to mate has abolished courtship, chivalry, tenderness, love itself'.

Fortunately, Dr. Poole, a bachelor at thirty-eight, arrives in time for the annual orgy. Unfortunately, he is the typical Huxley male (such as Rivers in *The Genius and the Goddess* or Jeremy Pordage in *After Many a Summer Dies the Swan*), a man who was bullied by his mother and is still intimidated by his own desires. He 'has spent half a lifetime surreptitiously burning'. He has never been able to bring himself to do what the eighteen-year-old Loola and her society must force themselves to stop. Neither he nor she, as representatives of their respective societies, can manage physical and emotional relationships. Neither the unlimited intercourse of *Brave New World*, an extreme extension of the new sexual freedom of the 1920s, nor the total repression of *Ape and Essence*, a novel whose society is as anti-love as that of *1984*, can produce the balance of body and mind sought by Philip and Elinor Quarles in *Point Counter Point*. In the course of the annual orgy, however, Alfred Poole and Loola discover in each other something akin to old-fashioned love. This is, however, an odd event, even in a distopia, from which to date one's hopes for a better humanity and it is here the novel's major weakness lies. Out of this ludicrous couple Huxley must create the future of the human race. He must transform Alfred Poole from Denis Stone of *Crome Yellow* into Anthony Beavis of *Eyeless in Gaza*.

Although the transformation does take place, it is hardly credible. Loola's vapid 'Alfie, I believe I shall never want to say Yes to anyone except you' is followed by the Narrator's overwritten reflection:

> And so, by the dialectic of sentiment, these two have rediscovered for themselves that synthesis of the chemical and the personal, to which we give the names of monogamy and romantic love. In her case it was the hormone that excluded the person; in his, the person that could not come to terms with the hormone. But now there is the beginning of a larger wholeness.

Loola escapes the sheer animalism of the mating season and Alfred becomes more human as a result of having behaved like an animal. A sort of balance is restored by the pair and in each of its members. The larger wholeness, the re-ascent to the human level and the possibilities beyond it, becomes the main concern in the scant thirty pages of the novel that remain.

But the novel itself lacks wholeness. Huxley's attempt to blend farce and high seriousness seldom succeeds. Each element works individually as long as one does not think of the other. The scene in which Alfred, several days after the orgy, when constraint is again the rule, cautiously advances towards Loola and the scavengers 'from behind the tomb of Rudolf Valentino' is quite successful. So too with Poole's epiphanic realization, as though he were Anthony Beavis or Sebastian Barnack, of the supernatural reality underlying appearances. But it is impossible to believe these two events involve the same man. Admittedly, in one of his earliest appearances, Poole's intelligence was said to be 'potential, his attractiveness no more than latent', but Shelleyan and mystical tendencies were hardly apparent.

Nevertheless, it is with Shelley and his semi-mystical poetry that Huxley, through Poole's search for the 'larger wholeness', makes his peace in *Ape and Essence*. In *Those Barren Leaves*, Chelifer classified Shelley's poetry as escapism (Part 2, I) and in *Point Counter Point*, apparently with Huxley's approval, Rampion defined Shelley as a poet filled with 'a bloodless kind of slime' (X). Yet when Poole wishes to dissuade Loola from her allegiance to the restrictive sexual customs practised by the society of *Ape and Essence*, he begins to quote from the volume of Shelley he rescued from the bakery oven in much the same fashion that Huxley salvaged Tallis' script from the incinerator. Thirty-four years earlier, in *Point Counter Point*, Burlap, and not the hero, would be behaving in this manner. 'We shall become the same, we shall be one / Spirit within two frames, oh! Wherefore two?' Poole asks, quoting *Epipsychidion*. He realizes that making love like human beings 'mightn't always and everywhere be the right thing. But here and now it is—definitely.'

It is a limited ideal, Huxley feels, though it is superior to that held by the rest of society in *Ape and Essence*. Beyond it, perhaps because of it, Poole already perceives something higher. The Narrator perceives it too and asks: 'is there already the beginning of an understanding that beyond *Epipsychidion* there is *Adonais* and beyond *Adonais*, the wordless doctrine of the Pure in Heart?' Presumably so, since the novel concludes with Poole quoting the next to last stanza (54) of *Adonais* in which, for Huxley, the 'Light whose smile kindles the Universe' is 'The fire for which all thirst' or, in other words, the mystic's Divine Ground.

As the novel ends, Loola and Poole are on their way to join an isolated community of 'Hots' near Fresno, a group of individuals too combustible to conform to society's strictures on sex. The Arch-Vicar previously described this settlement to Poole. It is the 'community of exiles' the Savage had no chance to seek. And though it seems preoccupied with sex and may never have heard of 'man's Final End', Poole is now potentially capable of explaining it to them. Soon enough the 'Hots' may find themselves transformed into the Vedanta Society of Southern California.

One recalls that *Ape and Essence* began with a meeting of two scriptwriters, one of whom is presumably Huxley himself, on the day of Gandhi's assassination. It ends with the emergence, in Tallis' film script, of a new religious leader, thus confirming the incipient mystic Alfred Poole's own statement that the 'Order of Things' always reasserts itself, even if it requires centuries. The description Huxley gives in the opening pages of the novel of Gandhi's Indians 'governing themselves, village by village, and worshipping the Brahman who is also Atman' is perhaps meant as a forecast of the future in store for the 'Hots'. Oddly enough, Gandhi was labelled a reactionary, whereas, according to Sebastian Barnack's outline of life as a progression into the world of spiritual eternity, he was spiritually in the forefront of evolutionary development. Nevertheless, any implied comparison between Alfred Poole and Mahatma Gandhi only accentuates the former's failure to move convincingly from comic butt to mystic hero.

IV

Huxley's final work of fiction, *Island*, is not only a point by point reply to *Brave New World* but a successful replay of an opportunity bungled by society in *Ape and Essence*. The Arch-Vicar, pleased to be living in the worst of possible worlds, admits it almost became the best. If Eastern mysticism and Western science had only modified one another, says the Arch-Vicar, if Eastern art had refined Western energy while Western individualism tempered Eastern totalitarianism, 'it would have been the kingdom of heaven'. Whereas the devil-worshipping Arch-Vicar 'shakes his head in pious horror' at the thought of such a utopia, Huxley attempts to bring it to life in *Island*.

Perhaps the central fact behind Pala's survival and success in a hostile world is the union of East and West it represents. It is thus, as Philip Quarles would be pleased to note, a blend of contrasting viewpoints out of which a total picture has resulted. The novel relates how Dr. Andrew MacPhail, stranded in India in the late nineteenth century, was hastily summoned to Pala to treat its Raja for an apparently incurable tumour (VII). Drawing on the revolutionary 'animal magnetism' techniques of a certain Professor Elliotson, MacPhail effects an impossible cure and stays on as a sort of prime minister. The Scottish doctor and the Palanese king, 'the Calvanist-turned atheist and the pious Mahayana Buddust', represent Western knowledge and Eastern religion. They are a pair 'of complementary temperaments', Huxley writes, and they soon teach one another 'to make the best of both worlds— the Oriental and the European, the ancient and the modern'. Unlike Denis and Mary in *Crome Yellow* or Lord Edward and Webley in *Point Counter Point*, the doctor and the Raja are not parallel lines each of which ignores the other's viewpoint. Neither finds his outlook, whether scientific or religious, completely sufficient. Instead, the pair bring about what Huxley considers the perfect synthesis. They accomplish a fusion that the Arch-Vicar would deplore but which every Vedantist believes is the key to a utopian future.

To the West Swami Vivekananda and the Ramakrishna Order of Vedanta preached the need for spiritual experience. To the East they recommended social improvements and Western know-how. For the Vedantist, the perennial philosophy of Vedanta is 'a potential bridge between science and religion' because its notion of a higher form of consciousness, called God or Brahman, underlying the world's diversity, is 'largely in accord with the latest theories of astronomy and atomic physics'. Pala is the Vedantist's paradise, a working out in fiction of what Huxley and his mystic-oriented co-religionists feel is the best possible programme for tomorrow. Modern Pala, as a society, holds to the perennial philosophy. Where William Morris presented a nation of medieval craftsmen, Huxley offers an island of mystics. The society composed entirely of Alphas that Mustapha Mond of *Brave New World* says failed miserably (XVI), here succeeds. The Palanese are of many different capacities intellectually, but they are all Alphas spiritually; and not even the sham mystics, such as the Rani or the industrialist, Joe Aldehyde, can offset their attractiveness.

Mysticism and utopian thought are less far apart than one might suppose. Where the latter wishes to build the best possible civilization in this world, the former insists that one can have a taste of eternal life while still in the temporal–physical order. Both seek to transform the present into their respective ideas of what constitutes its most elevated state. >From Huxley's earlier point of view, however, the writer of the Wells or Bellamy caliber is entertaining a 'compensatory dream', an unrealizable and unnecessary ideal, whereas the Huxley of *Island* is neither dreaming nor contradicting his earlier self. The myna birds that cover Pala and keep repeating 'Attention', 'here and now', or 'Compassion', are continual reminders that one must seek the ultimate reality of union with the Divine Ground. Ultimate reality, which countless mystics claim to have experienced, cannot be synonymous, Huxley would no doubt contend, with compensatory dream.

What *Island* represents is Huxley's heroic attempt to reconcile science, sex, and religion, three items that have always been at odds in all of his fiction, especially the previous utopias. *Brave New World* was built by the first and the happiness of its inhabitants depended on an unlimited supply of the second, but religion was essentially absent. *Ape and Essence* contained a society that was destroyed by science and that had, as a result, perverse forms of religion and sex. Perhaps it is more correct to say Huxley, in *Island*, is endeavouring to create a religious society wherein both science and sex—

towards each of which he has certain antipathies—will have an undisputed place. His method of integrating these three elements is to make both science and sex somewhat religious. Thus Dr. MacPhail, the direct descendant of Dr. Andrew, personifies the two strains that originally went into the making of Pala and is a physician-scientist as well as a virtual guru to the visiting Will Farnaby. And the Palanese practice *maithuna* (VI) or 'the yoga of love', in which the goal is as much spiritual as physical, a combination of mystical awareness and sensual satisfaction.

What is less easy to detect (but no less relevant) is that Huxley has also made religion somewhat scientific and sensual. In *The Mystics of the Church*, Evelyn Underhill once defined mysticism as 'the science of the Love of God' and Vedanta unabashedly insists mysticism is a sort of experiment wherein, if one follows the teaching of past mystics, one can approach by determinable stages to a knowledge of the Infinite. Indeed, the moksha-medicine that Will takes (a commendable replacement for the escapist drug, soma, in *Brave New World*) gives him what Huxley himself, in *Heaven and Hell*, claims to have had: a scientifically-induced spiritual experience that Huxley believes to be genuine, even if the more traditional-minded students of mysticism would object. The Palanese call this drug the 'reality revealer', the 'truth-and-beauty-pill' (IX). The scientific validity and indestructability of this mystic experience is asserted by Will in an almost Gradgrindian manner: 'the fact remained and would remain always ... the fact that the ground of all being could be totally manifest ... the fact that there was a light and that this light was also compassion' (XV).

The ultimate scientific sanction, however, is Huxley and Sebastian Barnack's notion that mystic awareness is the eventual goal of the evolutionary process, that one moves from animal eternity to time to spiritual eternity. The Vedanta-oriented essays of Christopher Isherwood and Swami Prabhavananda overflow with similar assurances, as do those of Gerald Heard. Heard insists that 'the end of evolution is not the creation of bigger and more complicated societies and more elaborate economic structures but the attainment of a higher and intenser form of consciousness'. Sexually, the union with the Divine Ground is celebrated by mystics such as Jacob Boehme and St. John of the Cross as a fusion more intense and liberating than any purely physical experience. It results, Huxley contends, in a loss of self and a simultaneous accession of being that are incomparably greater than any two lovers, even the Birkin and Ursula of *Women in Love*, whom Huxley once admired, can attain.

Huxley's utopian trilogy also involves three different attempts by society to cope with Huxley's (and the Vedantist's) primary enemy: the ego.

Mustapha Mond's society sanctioned a false escape from the narrowness of egotism by encouraging unlimited fornication and soma holidays. Only in a physical sense does everyone belong to everyone else. The society that bravely survives in *Ape and Essence* spurred on its own downfall by opposing the ego to the Order of Things. Only *Island*, as a society of mystics, has found the way to transcend the ego, to discover, as did Anthony Beavis in *Eyeless in Gaza*, the Atman in each individual. More so than any other utopia, Pala claims to be a bridge between this world and the next, to be, almost literally, heaven on earth.

Even more important to Huxley than the fusion of science, sex, and religion, however, is the attempt in *Island* to rewrite *Brave New World*, to redress the picture of the future he previously offered with one that is positive and Vedantic. Viewed from the vantage point of *Island*, in which many of the questions Huxley raised in 1932 are revived and updated, *Brave New World* is seen as a society that confronted the right problems but with the wrong answers. *Island* is also an effort to consolidate ideas previously expressed in numerous essays, such as those in *Ends and Means* (1937), *The Perennial Philosophy* (1945), *Tomorrow and Tomorrow and Tomorrow* (1956), and *Brave New World Revisited* (1958). Huxley is bent on showing how all of his previous recommendations, both social and moral, coalesce into a viable whole. *Island* is truly the summation of most of Huxley's writing since *Brave New World*.

There is scarcely an event, attitude, or programme in *Brave New World* that does not find what Huxley considers its more commendable counterpart in *Island*. The needs and trends from which *Brave New World* resulted must be reconciled with Vedanta or Huxley's own life and thought will be split and disconnected. Thus where the Director of Hatcheries and Conditioning uses hypnopaedia (sleep-teaching) (II), a Palanese educator, Mrs. Narayan, implements a system that teaches short cuts to memorizing: 'One starts by learning how to experience twenty seconds as ten minutes, a minute as half an hour' (XIII). The children are taught a method of speed-learning instead of being brain-washed in their sleep. The method is as much spiritual as educational since it gives the practitioner a means of escaping briefly from time and space limitations, a taste, as it were, of the eternal.

Nowhere in Pala is specialization or narrowness condoned in any form. A major rule of Palanese education is 'Never give children a chance of imagining that anything exists in isolation', teach them 'Balance, give and take, no excesses' because 'it's the rule in nature' (XIII). Every course the children take 'is punctuated by periodical bridge-building sessions' (XIII) that Paul de Vries of *Time Must Have a Stop* would envy. Quarles wished to present reality from all the 'various aspects—emotional, scientific, economic, religious, metaphysical' (XXII); and every subject in Palanese schools is considered 'as a fact of aesthetic or spiritual experience as well as in terms of science or history or economics'. What Quarles recommends in *Point Counter Point*, the Palanese practice. For them, a confrontation between the scientist, Lord Edward, and the politician, Webley, could not result in mutually impenetrable viewpoints.

Where the Deltas and Epsilons of *Brave New World* are animated Pavlovian experiments trained to do one job only, the Palanese are thoroughly familiar with Jung's theories about psychological types and with the Sheldonian classifications Huxley admires. Pala provides the way of devotion for extroverts, the way of self-knowledge for introverts, and the way of disinterested action for muscular, athletic individuals (XIII). Children are divided into groups by temperament and then into a given group, such as that of introverts, some extroverts and muscle-men are introduced. Tolerance is encouraged. *Brave New World*, by contrast, was the logical outcome, engineered by science, of the society seen in all of Huxley's early novels: a society of egoists each of whom could only tolerate his own one-pointed preoccupation and lived in a private world. *Island* is thus an attempt to abolish the targets Huxley has satirized throughout his novels. The Palanese oppose their openness to the many forms of narrowness and exclusiveness Mustapha Mond's society thrived on. Even as adults, the Palanese are forced to specialize as little as possible and then only in the jobs (not job) best suited to their talents. Though he laughed at the idea when it appeared in Wells, Huxley has the Palanese exchange jobs repeatedly, moving, as in Vijaya Bhattacharya's case, from a scientific lab to a position chopping wood.

A complete list of parallel situations in *Brave New World* and *Island* would cover several pages. The Solidarity Service in *Brave New World* (V), for example, and the Purification Day ceremonies of *Ape and Essence* are unsatisfactory variations of the ritual in which young Palanese get their first taste of the moksha-medicine (X). Where the infantile adults of *Brave New World* play Centrifugal Bumble-puppy and the children indulge in rudimentary sexual games, Palanese youngsters receive a sound sexual training. The rather adult infants of Pala also play such informative but possibly boring games as Psychological Bridge and Evolutionary Snakes and Ladders (XIII).

The scene in *Brave New World* wherein Linda, the Savage's mother, dies from soma addiction in the midst of indifferent death-conditioned youngsters is balanced by the death of Dr. MacPhail's wife in *Island*. The Palanese are also death-conditioned, but for them this means being prepared to 'go on practising the art of living even while they're dying' (XIV). Like the deceased Eustace Barnack in *Time Must Have a Stop*, the dying Lakshmi is conscious of the presence of a light. She, however, does not refuse to be absorbed into it. The entire death scene, including Susila MacPhail's advice to the dying woman, is almost a direct dramatization of the moment of death as described in the 'Tibetan Book of the Dead'.

Huxley was not satirizing the society of *Brave New World* for tampering with the family, using drugs to expand consciousness, or for controlling the breeding process. Nor was he opposed to taking the utmost care in matching the individual with the position most suited to his capabilities. The Palanese do all these things, but in a manner Huxley can approve of because it is neither impersonally scientific nor inhumanly mechanical. It is all done by humane means in the light of what Huxley takes to be man's Final End, not to promote a stagnant hedonism such as that of Mustapha Mond's world. Vijaya and Shanta's youngest child, for example, is the product of artificial insemination and should have some of the characteristics of his real father, the painter Gobind Singh (XII). The artist has been dead for years, but his seed has been preserved by a process called, somewhat grotesquely, Deep Freeze. By similar experiments in eugenics, the practical Palanese plan to raise their average IQ to 115 within a century. Although science and the centralized government of brave new world society were hand in hand, it is the decentralized world of MacPhail, foreshadowed in 'Centralization and Decentralization' in *Ends and Means*, that seems to have co-ordinated science and unlimited progress.

Huxley was not totally unsympathetic to the unfavourable opinion that *Brave New World* had of motherhood and family life. His novels show he regards both as possible barriers to the child's development. Jeremy Pordage of *After Many a Summer Dies the Swan*, Rivers of *The Genius and the Goddess*, and even Mark Rampion in *Point Counter Point* suffered under domineering mothers. Murugan, the future Raja of Pala, is also the victim of possessive motherhood in the person of the Rani. Pala, however, has what Huxley considers a saner solution to the inadequacies of the family system in its Mutual Adoption Clubs, an arrangement not unlike the revision of the family Plato advocated in Book V of his *Republic*. Any child in difficulty at home (or causing difficulty) can temporarily move or be moved into any of the other nineteen families in the club his family belongs to (VII). This prevents parental tyranny and discourages the formation of strong family ties on anything but a wide, social basis. Mustapha Mond talked of older societies as being exclusive and narrow, but the Palanese family system, like all of Pala, is, in Susila MacPhail's words, 'not exclusive ... but inclusive.'

Thus in many respects the ends of *Brave New World* society and those of Pala are similar, but the all-important means are invariably different. Both societies have heard Malthus' warnings, but Pala does not respond by severing all connection between sex and procreation. Throughout *Island* Huxley attempts to reconsider the trends he uncovered in *Brave New World* and come up with answers to them that he and his fellow Vedantists will be able to live with.

Huxley's first two utopias are therefore extensions of previous visions. *Brave New World* is the society of mutually intolerant egotists in Huxley's first four novels pushed to its logical extreme. The world of *Ape and Essence* is an extension of the simian existence of Jo Stoyte and the Fifth Earl in *After Many a Summer Dies the Swan*. Yet *Island* is not really a universalization of the wisdom attained by Anthony Beavis in *Eyeless in Gaza*. Although Huxley's first utopia deals with England and the second with America, the third is literally nowhere. It is much more imaginary and it is not world-wide. Huxley could comfortably predict the destruction of Europe and America, but at the end of his life, could only foresee social and spiritual salvation for small, isolated communities. Outside these communities, surrounding them, the worlds of Mustapha Mond and the Arch-Vicar still exist. As Bahu, Rendang's ambassador, realizes, Pala can stay alive only as long as it remains deliberately out of touch with the rest of the contaminated world (v). Huxley's essays, such as 'Ozymandias, the Utopia that Failed' in *Tomorrow and Tomorrow and Tomorrow*, reveal his preoccupation with small, marginal groups (monasteries, Quaker settlements) and indicate that *Island* is possibly the only literary utopia partially based on what its author learned from actual utopian experiments past and present. But where many previous utopias, when not world-wide, felt certain they could exercise a beneficial influence, Pala regards the rest of the world as an encroaching insane asylum.

Only to readers familiar with Huxley's two previous utopias and with his perennial concerns will his final, Herculean attempt at resolution and synthesis be fully apparent. But although Pala is the only one of Huxley's utopias, and possibly the only positive literary utopia, that one would choose to live in, *Island*, considered as a work of literature, is scarcely successful. It resolves the problems faced by Huxley's previous utopian societies but it contains, as literature, nearly all the flaws of positive utopias mentioned earlier in the discussion of affirmative and negative utopias. The book is a novel only by courtesy of definition. It brings Huxley's life-long struggle with the dramatic requirements of the novel, even if one amends this to discussion-novel-of-ideas, to an unsuccessful conclusion. Its plot, wherein Will gradually discovers Pala's value and is in the midst of his first mystical experience at the moment Col. Dipa of Rendang stages his military coup, is the book's weakest aspect. This is the only novel of ideas Huxley wrote in which the plot gets in the way of ideas that are sufficiently interesting in themselves and that suffer from indifferent dramatization.

It is hard to believe in the efficacy of Pala's system when the plot of the novel shows the Palanese failing to convert (or at least neutralize) Murugan, their future Raja. The young man remains an unshaken egoist (V), fails to respond to sex education, is a latent homosexual and the victim of his mother's sham spiritualism. He becomes an unintentional symbol of human nature's ability to become perverse despite the influence of the most ideal environment. In a society of non-attached people, his favourite reading is a Sears, Roebuck and Co. catalogue (IX). He insists he will 'get this place modernized' (V) as soon as he is old enough to rule. He reminds one of a Sebastian Barnack who will never grow up.

No genuinely religious society, however utopian and pacifist, would tolerate the Rani's plans to lease Pala's hitherto unworked oil concessions to the caricature of a capitalist that Huxley calls Joe Aldehyde. Murugan's mother, the Rani, fully intends to ruin a utopia to finance her so-called 'Crusade of the Spirit', a movement that is supposed to 'save Humanity from self-destruction' (V). In a society of fully developed mystics, she recalls Mr. Barbacue-Smith of *Crome Yellow* with his *Pipe-Lines to the Infinite*. It is impossible to believe the Rani can be as blind as Huxley makes her or that her society is willing to let her persist in her blindness.

With the aid of Col. Dipa of nearby Rendang, Murugan illegally assumes power before his eighteenth birthday. His and his mother's dream of a Westernized, materialistic country seems about to come true. The Palanese, as pacifists, offer no resistance and Dr. MacPhail is summarily shot. While it is abundantly clear that each of Huxley's last two utopias is written with its predecessor in mind, it is not certain that Pala is to be the final variation. The goals of Col. Dipa and the desires of Murugan seem likely to produce Mustapha Mond's world all over again if they do not produce the Arch-Vicar's first. Murugan advocates 'an intensive programme of industrialization' to make insecticides, for 'If you can make insecticides, you can make nerve gas' (V). One recollects that the two rival armies of baboons in *Ape and Essence* destroyed each other with a type of gas called 'plague-fog'.

If one recalls the smugness of certain Palanese—such as eighteen-year-old Nurse Apu discussing the spiritual quality of orgasms (VI)—the destruction of Pala becomes less difficult to bear. A society in which the ability to practice advanced psychology extends to all the inhabitants including the children cannot be consistently appealing. One is tempted to equate Pala, despite its spiritual maturity, with a magnified Boy Scout Camp, just as *Brave New World* was an enlarged assembly line. The unflagging attention each person pays to his own mental and spiritual development while prescribing for that of all around him seems almost neurotic. The formulas and injections given the bottle-babies in *Brave New World* are haphazard by comparison. Yet Pala does personify a life-style more complete than that found in most positive utopias prior to Huxley's, even if much of Pala's success is explained or simply asserted rather than depicted. As Col. Dipa's tanks roll in, the contrast between what is being destroyed and what will take its place does more than certain parts of the novel can to increase our admiration for Pala. The synthesis of East and West that Vedanta and Huxley both call for is ironically destroyed by the East's desire to become as imperialistic and materialistic as the modern West.

By destroying his own utopia, however, Huxley does not necessarily reveal himself as a cynical salvationist. Usually, the utopia remains and the visitor is somehow forced to return to his own time (as in Morris). Here, Will Farnaby's own time overtakes both him and Pala simultaneously. But the myna birds come out again after the tanks have passed and resume their cries of 'Attention.' The pacifist, Vedantic Palanese will never become the standing army Murugan desires. Pala is no less real now than it was throughout the novel as a province of Huxley's mind. Its very fragility in the face of Dipa's assault is a sort of guarantee to Wiley that it is no charmed, compensatory fantasy but rather a realizable ideal. It is the type of society that the militaristic and materialistic world of Col. Dipa would regard as a genuine threat and which, regardless of its vulnerability, Huxley and Vedanta feel should be the goal for the future.

Despite Pala, however, *Brave New World* remains Huxley's most convincing picture of the future and his best blending of utopian concerns with novelistic format. *Brave New World* is also Huxley's most plausible excuse for writing *Island* as a corrective vision, even if many readers will regard the latter as his 'compensatory dream'.

GEORGE WOODCOCK

Destructive Encounters

1

Transitions, in history or in human lives, are rarely abrupt or clearly defined, and it is not the dark and dramatic satire of *Point Counter Point* that marks Huxley's abandonment of his preoccupations with the hinterland of Bohemia and the Monde in the immediate post-war years so much as his last volume of stories, *Brief Candles*, which appeared in the spring of 1930.

Brief Candles consists of three shorter stories and a novella, 'After the Fireworks'. The most persistent theme is the destructive encounter between the generations. The presence of that conflict is itself nothing new in Huxley's work. The theme is strong in earlier stories, especially 'Happily Ever After'. It is muted in *Crome Yellow*, *Antic Hay* and *Those Barren Leaves*. Henry Wimbush and Gumbril Senior may be dottily eccentric, but they are genially portrayed; Scogan and Cardan may at times seem tedious elderly bores, but usually they have some philosophic point to make that interests the reader and presumably the younger characters, who in general listen to them with respect. It is in the portrayal of women past their prime, like Priscilla Wimbush and Mrs. Aldwinkle, that malice becomes evident in these earlier novels, and it can be interpreted more plausibly as an example of Huxley's chronic misogyny than of hostility towards an elder generation. Generally speaking, in the first three novels, it is mainly among his own

From *Dawn and the Darkest Hour: A Study of Aldous Huxley*. © 1972 by George Woodcock.

contemporaries, the men and women spoilt by direct or indirect participation in the war and growing up in its shadow, that Huxley is inclined to find his more unpleasant characters. In *Point Counter Point* the criticism of the older generation has sharpened. In developing the character of John Bidlake, Huxley makes rather brutally the point that a selfishness acceptable in a young man of charm and talent is no longer so in an ageing artist whose best work lies in the past. And in the elder Quarles, viewed with contempt by his own son, we have the young ne'er-do-well grown old, and trapped in a sordid generation-cum-caste situation by his abduction of a young typist.

When, after *Point Counter Point*, the theme of the generations is persistently repeated in *Brief Candles*, it seems clear that Huxley's preoccupation is connected with his own growing sense of passing out of youth. He was thirty-five when he collected the stories in *Brief Candles*, and that, as Cardan told Calamy, is the first of the great climacterics. He was conscious of advancing middle age, conscious also that this advance was accompanied by fundamental changes in the self who had written his first four novels. It must have been obvious to him, even as he completed it, that he could never write another dark masterpiece like *Point Counter Point*, and we may see 'After the Fireworks', the most important piece in *Brief Candles*, as Huxley's farewell to the literary life as he had experienced it up to this time, the life of the novelist as distinct from the teacher who, with *Brave New World*, finally assumes the ascendancy.

'Chawdron', the first story in *Brief Candles*, is interesting for the various anticipations of Huxley's future writing which it brings together. Chawdron himself, the ruthless financier hero, is the prototype of Joe Stoyte, the crude entrepreneur who dominates *After Many a Summer*, and 'the Fairy', his tawdry little secretary with her spiritual airs, anticipates the promiscuous but pietistic Virginia Maunciple, who is Joe Stoyte's young mistress. But while Virginia holds Joe Stoyte by her physical charms, 'the Fairy' holds Chawdron by her power of deceiving herself into fake mystical states. Huxley treads at last those marginal lands of the spiritual life inhabited by the genuine mystics of his later novels, but also by the victims of possession and false spirituality portrayed in *Grey Eminence* and *The Devils of Loudun*.

'Chawdron' is constructed in the Conradian manner, as a dialogue taking place at the time of Chawdron's death between the anonymous narrator and a failed writer named Tilney—a kind of grand might-have-been like Cardan—who has written a single masterpiece. It is the book that passes as Chawdron's autobiography; the canny old financier succeeded in suppressing the evidence of its real authorship so effectively that Tilney has in fact no monument to his own talents. In any case, he wrote it mainly for money, to support his love affair with Sybil, a 'pale-eyed, pale-haired ghost' of Huxley's Circean type. The shadowy Sybil ends a drug-addict, and in her degeneration anticipates Mary Amberley, the mistress of Anthony Beavis in *Eyeless in Gaza*. More than that, Sybil's addiction marks the beginning of a growing interest in drugs, and their effects on the human personality and human perceptions, that remains with Huxley from this point to his death, eventually changing in its direction, like his interests in mysticism and in Utopias, from negative to positive.[1]

If 'Chawdron' looks forward to Huxley's later works, 'The Rest Cure' returns to one of the strands of *Antic Hay*, for Moira Tarwin adventuring in Italy is an elaboration of Rosie Shearwater adventuring in London; both are wives of scientists, and both find disillusionment in what they imagine is romance. While Rosie's experiences tend to the farcical, Moira's have a hysterical intensity that is bound to end in tragedy. She exemplifies the fact—which Huxley observed mingling with the English residents in Italy—that: 'One of the pleasures or dangers of foreign travel is that you lose your class-consciousness.'

With Moira it is more than a loss of class-consciousness; she lacks the experience that enables her to judge character with ease, and she is so ready for a change from the detested John Tarwin that she falls easily for the cheap charms of the small-hotel-keeper's son, Tonino. As Moira becomes impassioned, Tonino's interest cools. There is a final scene in which, after he has gone, Moira misses her handbag and thinks he has stolen it. Believing that he has made love to her merely for her money, she shoots herself. Then comes a last sardonic twist in the manner of Maupassant. As the servants arrange the bed to lay her out, the bag falls to ground; it had lodged between the bed and the wall.

This bitter exemplary tale is the best of the shorter stories in *Brief Candles*. 'The Claxtons', which follows it, is an excessive attack on the sandal-wearing vegetarian cultists who were regarded as fair game by English satirists in the 1930s; it is also a depressing study of the way a human will can be destroyed. The plot centres on the struggle of wills between Martha Claxton and her sullen, wilful and unattractive daughter Sylvia. Sylvia is finally made tractable by the kindness of her aunt Judith, who reveals to her a life that seems rich in experience after the austerities of home, and when she returns to the country cottage where the Claxtons pursue their lives as minor artists, she is vulnerable, her rebellion breaks down, and she becomes the dull tool of her mother's will. The real interest of 'The Claxtons' lies in its revelation of the shedding of Lawrence's influence. For Herbert and Martha Claxton are the other side of the Rampions—a rich girl marrying a

poor man, setting out to live the balanced life of creativity and spiritual
fulfilment, and in this case ending in hypocrisy and moral tyranny. This is
only one of the ironic allusions to Lawrence in *Brief Candles*; Moira's
surrender to the lower-class Tonino reminds one of *Lady Chatterley's Lover*,
while in 'After the Fireworks' one of the characters claims attention, like
Lady Chatterley herself, for an affair with a gamekeeper.

'After the Fireworks' exists on quite a different level of complexity from
the shorter stories. Like 'Uncle Spencer' and 'Two or Three Graces', it is a
novella that deserves the greater attention it would have gained from
separate publication, and, like them, it differs from Huxley's larger novels
(with the exception of *Eyeless in Gaza*) in presenting an intensive
psychological study of one human being in a special predicament.

The hint from which 'After the Fireworks' developed came from
Huxley's reading of Chateaubriand's letters.

> When he was sixty [Huxley told a correspondent] a very young
> girl at a watering place came and threw herself at his head. He
> wrote her a most exquisite letter, which is extant. And there the
> matter ended, even though she did invade his house one evening.
> With my usual sadism, I thought it would be amusing to give it
> the cruel ending. And as one couldn't use Chateaubriand
> himself—that monstrous pride and loneliness and, underneath
> the burning imagination, that emotional aridity would have been
> impracticable to handle—I made the hero one of those people
> (they have always fascinated me and provoked a certain envy) who
> know how to shirk natural consequences and get something for
> nothing, give Nemesis the slip.

There is more in the story than this summary suggests, and the final
impression it leaves is not that the hero has given 'Nemesis the slip'; to the
contrary, in fact. Miles Fanning is a successful novelist who has specialized in
romantic stories of liberated young women. An elegantly ageing man, he
contrives to give an impression of unworn vitality that conceals his real
condition. It is his curious fate to be entrapped in one of the situations he
loves to invent in fiction.

Pamela Tarn—her very name that of a heroine in cheaply romantic
fiction—writes to Fanning, and then waylays him in Rome. She is twenty-
one, and juvenile for her age; Miles is charmed with her prettiness and her
evident adoration. He starts out with a kind of avuncular patronage, but both
he and Pamela are the victims of their delusions; she is deceived by the air of

the romantic man of letters which he projects, and he by the manner of a character out of one of his novels which she has assumed.

It soon becomes evident that Pamela intends to follow the routine of a Fanning novel and be seduced by the writer-hero. Realizing this, Fanning debates flight, but Pamela frustrates his plans of secret departure. She becomes his mistress, and the experience on both sides is a shedding of illusion, a learning, through sheer physical experience, what a love affair between a vain, ageing man and a sentimental, immature girl actually means.

Pamela's first lesson comes when she realizes that life with a romantic writer is not romantic; he is so absorbed with fictional people while he is at work that the real ones have little meaning for him. Here, seen by the victim, is the problem of the atrophy of human feelings that Philip Quarles in *Point Counter Point* viewed as a writer.

But it is—typically—in sickness with its grotesque reminders of physical decay, that Huxley teaches his characters the ultimate lesson of the folly of romantic expectations. In the spring of 1929 Huxley had suffered from an acute liver ailment and had visited the great spa at Montecatini with its '750 hotels and pensions'. He was fascinated by the macabre comedy of the scene, the parade of 'the obese, the bilious, the gluttons', including 'a high percentage of priests, who flock thither in black swarms to drink off the effects of the proverbial clerical overeating'. The final scenes of 'After the Fireworks' take place in this grim but ludicrous setting, for Fanning is jaundiced because of a chill on the liver brought on by sexual excesses with Pamela which his ageing body has not been able to sustain. As the story ends, Pamela is about to leave him for a younger man. Romance in real life is an illusion.

'After the Fireworks' marks Huxley's rejection of the role of the novelist as artist, his farewell to the dilettantish pursuit of pure art and pure knowledge. For Fanning, though he is not recognizably a self-portrait, represents Huxley's inclination to become immersed in aesthetic and scholarly interests. When he remarks: 'That's the definition of culture—knowing and thinking about things that have absolutely nothing to do with us,' he is expressing an attitude Huxley now wishes to repudiate. Yet, while it is a final rejecting look at the past, 'After the Fireworks' is also, in a curiously inverted way, prophetic of the future. For Fanning's *past* in some ways anticipates Huxley's *future*; he has played with drugs, though less fatally than Sybil in 'Chawdron'; he has been 'quite perversely preoccupied with mystical experiences and ecstasies and private universes'. And, of more immediate interest at this stage in Huxley's development, it is Fanning who sees that link between Plato and 'Henry Ford and the machines', which will be developed in *Brave New World*.

2

Other events, as well as the publication of *Brief Candles*, mark the years of 1930 and 1931 as a climacteric period in Huxley's life. The spring of 1930 was clouded by the death of Lawrence. For at least two years Huxley had been painfully aware of the deterioration in his friend's health, though he had been amazed at the brightness with which the spirit's flame burnt in that body wasted by sickness. In January 1930, when he was living at Suresnes, Huxley learnt that Lawrence had entered a sanatorium at Vence, and towards the end of February he and Maria set off to visit him. They arrived to find him struggling with death. Huxley was present when Lawrence slipped into the last morphine sleep from which he never awoke.

> He gave one [Huxley told Eugene Saxton] the impression that he was living by sheer force of will and by nothing else. But the dissolution of the body was breaking down the will.... He was really, I think, the most extraordinary and impressive human being I have ever known.

Immediately, at Frieda Lawrence's invitation, Huxley began to collect Lawrence's letters and prepare them for publication. During 1930 and 1931 this was one of the tasks that most occupied his mind, and the very process of encountering in the letters aspects of his friend of which he was unaware led him to revise his views both of Lawrence and of the vitalism and primitivism which were essential to his beliefs. That process reached its conclusion during Huxley's visit to Mexico in 1933.

Meanwhile, in Europe, Huxley and Maria had drawn their Twenties to a geographical as well as a temporal end by abandoning the hinterland of the Italian Riviera, where his first four novels had all been written, and moving to France: at Sanary, near Bandol on the Côte d'Azur, they found a villa which reminded Huxley of the house of *Bouvard et Pecuchet*; 'a museum piece' as he told Robert Nichols, '—it seems almost a crime to alter and refurnish it.' Until their abandonment of Europe for the United States in 1937, the house at Sanary became their headquarters.

Here Huxley marked another break with the past by collecting his last volume of verse, *The Cicadas*, whose publication in 1931 was the virtual end of his career as a poet. His production of verse had been diminishing for a number of years, and the majority of the poems that make up *The Cicadas* had already appeared two years before in a smaller collection entitled *Arabia Infelix*; even the title poem, 'The Cicadas', belonged to that collection.

The earliest of these poems, 'Theatre of Varieties', dates from 1920, and the group of poems about the Roman emperors Nero and Caligula, which first appeared in *Those Barren Leaves* as the work of Francis Chelifer, must have been written before the completion of that novel in 1924. Of the two most important poems, 'Arabia Infelix' was published initially in 1926, and 'The Cicadas' in 1928. Most of the other poems were first published either in *Arabia Infelix* or in *The Cicadas*, but it is hard to date their composition; up to 1920 Huxley discussed his poems freely in his letters, but after that time he rarely even referred to them, a sign that his interest in poetry as an art was declining even when his poetic craftsmanship was becoming most accomplished.

Accomplishment, indeed, is the neutral quality that most distinguishes Huxley's later poems; they are smoother, more precise and economical than his earlier work, and, like everything he wrote, they make interesting statements. But they show the failure of development that occurs when a writer remains merely a craftsman, as Huxley did in poetry. There is no experimenting in form; the sonnet, the quatrain, the couplet, all in regular iambics, are Huxley's usual moulds. There is none of the complex use of allusiveness and parody which Eliot and Pound developed so effectively. And though, in imagery and at times in tone, Huxley is clearly influenced by the symbolists, he is not—as they were—seeking to establish his meaning by suggestion and indirection. He is, as much as Dryden, a poet of logical statement.

Much has been made of Huxley's French models, and there is no doubt that superficial characteristics were derived from the symbolists, from Laforgue, from Rimbaud, and from Baudelaire, a translation of whose poem on Lesbians, 'Femmes Damnées', appeared in *Arabia Infelix*. But the poems themselves as they emerge after the absorption of these influences are curiously English and even Victorian in their overt concern with the moral life of the author. In the group of sonnets about storms and tides that appears in *The Cicadas* one is left in no doubt that Huxley was Matthew Arnold's grand-nephew. For in few writers of the 1920s can one find such faithful echoes of Arnold as the final lines from the sonnet 'Mediterranean', which begins by evoking the gemlike sapphire that brims the tideless Tyrrhenian, and continues:

> *The ebb is mine. Life to its lowest neap*
> *Withdrawn reveals that black and hideous shoal*
> *Where I lie stranded. Oh deliver me*
> *From this defiling death! Moon of the soul,*

Call back the tide that ran so strong and deep,
Call back the shining jewel of the sea.

In a companion sonnet, 'Tide', Huxley envisages the tide for ever out, the sea retired past recall, and admonishes himself to a stoic resistance to despair.

There is a firm consenting to disaster,
Proud resignation to accepted pain.
Pain quickens him who makes himself its master,
And quickening battle crowns both loss and gain.
But to this silting of the soul, who gives
Consent is no more man, no longer lives.

This is not great or highly original poetry, but it is honest. Huxley is too conscientious to affect modernism for its own sake, to experiment without the creative passion that would give it meaning. He finds conventional verse, at this stage, a concise and effective way of expressing, through a mixture of metaphor and argument, his own mental condition. In the poems contained in *Cicadas* the storms that already ruffled the inner sea of his mind on the eve of his conversion are recorded, and there is an intense personal relevance to almost every poem, sometimes lightly disguised ('Arabia Infelix') and sometimes very directly stated ('The Cicadas').

'Arabia Infelix', probably inspired by watching the bare hot sands of the Yemeni desert from the boat to India in 1926, is a lyrical evocation of that arid land.

Parched, parched are the hills, and dumb
That thundering voice of the ravine;
Round the dead springs the birds are seen
No more, no more at evening come.

When the rain does come fleetingly to the dry hills of Arabia, the land awakens only briefly and in agony, for the cloud

Came laden with a gift of dew,
But with it dropped the lightning's flame;

A flame that rent the crags apart,
But rending made a road between
For water to the mountain's heart,
That left a scar, but left it green.

Faithless the cloud and fugitive;
An empty heaven nor burns, nor wets;
At peace, the barren land regrets
Those agonies that made it live.

It is a striking image, and its ultimate meaning lies in the creator's heart, but we are left in doubt whether the cloud means love or creativity or mystical insight. This perfectly achieved ambiguity makes 'Arabia Infelix' one of Huxley's most successful poems.

'The Cicadas', because it is more explicit, is at once a lesser poem and a more interesting personal document. For here the dilemma of death-orientation and life-orientation which was plaguing Huxley by 1928 is clearly stated and linked with his characteristic preoccupations regarding darkness and sight. The tone, Arnoldian to begin with, shifts by the end into a Wordsworthian key.

Huxley envisages himself standing in the Italian night. The first words of the poem echo back through his manhood into the blindness of adolescence.

Sightless, I breathe and touch; this night of pines
Is needly, resinous and rough with bark.
Through every crevice in the tangible dark,
The moonlessness above it all but shines.

Everything is still, but the stillness is that of continuous sound—the harsh and endless ringing of the cicadas.

I hear them sing, who in the double night
Of clouds and branches fancied that I went
Through my own spirit's dark discouragement,
Deprived of inward as of outward sight:

Who, seeking, even as here in the wild wood,
A lamp to beckon through my tangled fate,
Found only darkness and, disconsolate,
Mourned the lost purpose and the vanished good.

Now in my empty heart the crickets' shout
Re-echoing denies and still denies
With stubborn folly all my learned doubt,
In madness more than I in reason wise.

The madness of life that inspires the cicadas reawakens the poet's imagination, and, though he realizes that man's fate is still a moonless and 'labyrinthine night', from the knowledge of life's wonder he has learnt the value of desire that makes all experience new.

> *Clueless we go; but I have heard thy voice,*
> *Divine Unreason! harping in the leaves,*
> *And grieve no more; for wisdom never grieves,*
> *And thou hast taught me wisdom; I rejoice.*

The idea of sound as regenerative harks back to the time of Huxley's blindness, when music and the human voice took on special importance because they compensated for the loss of sight; sound in the darkness—like the 'music at night' which provides the title for Huxley's next book of essays—becomes a metaphor for enlightenment, though the enlightenment of 'The Cicadas' is not that which Huxley ultimately sought.

A complete study of Huxley's poems in relation to the development of his philosophic attitudes has never been made, and there is no room here to do more than hint at the importance of the elements of spiritual autobiography hidden under the bland and polished surface of these verses. The later poems—those written between 1929 and the publication of *The Cicadas* in 1931—are especially suggestive of the onset of deep and painful spiritual searching. Even more significant than the two Arnoldian sonnets in which the image of the ebbing tide is used to project an almost existentialist attitude of courageous hopelessness is 'The Moor', in which Iago, elevated as a model of orthodox Christian virtues, is shown being received into heaven. A more interesting fate—anticipating that of the later, mystical Huxley—awaits Othello.

> *Turning back meanwhile*
> *From outer darkness, Othello and his bride*
> *Perceive the globe of heaven like one small lamp*
> *Burning alone at midnight in the abyss*
> *Of some cathedral cavern; pause, and then*
> *With face once more averted, hand in hand,*
> *Explore the unseen treasures of the dark.*

3

If any vision runs more persistently than others through Huxley's works, from *Crome Yellow* in 1921 down to *Island* in 1962, it is that of Utopia, the world where a kind of perfection has been attained, change has come to a stop in a temporal parody of eternity. As a young man he saw Utopia as Hell on earth; as an old man he saw it as the earthly paradise. The difference between the two sides of the vision derives from a change in Huxley's views of human potentialities. For the greater part of his life he believed that only a tiny minority was capable of the highest thought or—in later years—of spiritual enlightenment, yet, apart from the brief period when he wrote *Proper Studies*, he distrusted the idea of a world which the elite planned for mankind as a whole. In his final years he believed that he had discovered the way, through mystical discipline and the intelligent use of drugs, to give every man an equal chance of an enlightened existence, and so a Utopia based on a balance of the physical and spiritual, the temporal and eternal, seemed possible to him; such was the vision he gave concrete form in *Island*.

Huxley's preoccupations with Utopias belong to a wider movement, for many writers in the earlier twentieth century were turning away from the facilely benign Utopias of the Renaissance and the nineteenth century. Some followed the example of Samuel Butler in *Erewhon* by creating negative Utopias, pictures of a future which, by reason of some flaw in human capabilities, has turned out to be the opposite of the ideal worlds that early socialists and early writers of science romance conceived. Even the most distinguished of the science romancers. H. G. Wells, balanced his positive Utopia *Men Like Gods* with the terrifyingly negative vision of *When the Sleeper Wakes*. Years before Huxley wrote *Brave New World*, E. M. Forster ('The Machine Stops') and Karel Čapek (*R.U.R.*) already portrayed in varying ways the withering of man's spiritual life and even of his physical capacities when he becomes too reliant on a machine-oriented world, and in 1924 there had appeared the first of the three great anti-Utopias of the twentieth century, Evgeny Zamiatin's *We*.

While *We* had a profound influence on the third of the key anti-Utopian novels, *1984*, its influence on *Brave New World* is obviously—if it exists—less profound and direct, despite the many striking resemblances between the two novels.

Both Huxley and Zamiatin see Utopia as a possible, even a probable outcome of twentieth-century technological developments, especially of the refinement of techniques in psychological suggestion. Both assume that in the process of creating Utopia man's outlook on life will be radically altered, since the stability necessary to maintain society unchanged will mean the elimination of the idea of freedom and the knowledge of the past; and the reduction of culture to a pattern of mechanical enjoyments. Both envisage the economic structure of Utopia as collectivist, and see its political structure as hierarchical, a pyramid topped by a tiny group of guardians who rule through effective police systems and conditioning techniques. They foresee the destruction of the very ideas of individuality and privacy, of passionate personal relationships, of any association outside the state. Both make happiness the goal of their Utopias, and equate it with non-freedom. Both use a passionless sexual promiscuity, based on the theory that each belongs to all, to break down any true intimacy between persons. The individual becomes an atom in the body of the state and nothing more. Even the rebellions in the two novels are alike, for in each case the hero—D.503 in *We* and Bernard Marx in *Brave New World*—is physically and mentally an atavistic throwback, and both heroes are tempted to rebellion by contact with men who have escaped the conditioning hand of the state: the hairy people who live outside the protective green wall of the Utopian city in *We*, the primitives of the New Mexican reservation in *Brave New World*. Needless to say, both rebellions fail; the unitary world utopian state continues on its course.

Striking as the resemblances may be, it is hard to prove that Huxley was influenced by Zamiatin at the time he wrote *Brave New World*. Unlike Orwell, he never admitted such an influence. And though, given Huxley's omnivorous reading habits, it seems unlikely that he failed to read *We* during the seven years between its publication and that of *Brave New World*, this appears to have affected only secondary details of his book. The essential outline of *Brave New World* was sketched already in *Crome Yellow*, and while it is true that *We* was written in 1920, and was secretly circulated as a forbidden text in Soviet Russia, it is improbable that Huxley saw a copy of it or even learnt of its existence before he conceived the character of Mr. Scogan and filled his mind with Utopian ideas.

The concept of Utopia, implicitly rejected in *Crome Yellow*, haunted Huxley as he watched the advance of the applied sciences and particularly of physiology and psychology. Utopia, he realized, was not entirely an impossible abstraction. Perhaps it cannot be made with men as they are. But science can change—if not men themselves—at least their attitudes and reactions, and then Utopia becomes feasible as a society in which men cease to be individuals and become merely the components of a social collectivity.

Utopia, of course, is a matter of imposing a pattern, of subordinating human life to a discipline of abstraction analogous to geometry. 'A mind impregnated with music', said Huxley in *Beyond the Mexique Bay*, 'will always tend to impose a pattern on the temporal flux.' But it seemed evident to him that any human attempt to impose an ideal order on Nature or on men would be perverted by man's limitations. So, for all his love of order in geometry and architecture and music, he distrusted it in political or social planning.

Brave New World marks a fundamental change in Huxley's use of the novel; it is no longer fiction intended to describe and satirize. The satirical element remains, but the primary function is now to exhort. Like Orwell's *1984*, *Brave New World* was deliberately devised as a cautionary tale. The earlier novels may have been didactic in part, as *Point Counter Point* clearly was whenever Rampion held the field; *Brave New World* is the first that will be didactic in total intent. This function of the novel, quite apart from any entertainment value it may have as a piece of futurist fantasy, is clearly stated in the description which Huxley gave his father in August 1931: he saw it as

> a comic, or at least satirical, novel about the Future, showing the appallingness (at any rate by our standards) of Utopia and adumbrating the effects on thought and feeling of such quite possible biological inventions as the production of children in bottles (with consequent, abolition of the family and all the Freudian 'complexes' for which family relationships are responsible), the prolongation of youth, the devising of some harmless but effective substitute for alcohol, cocaine, opium etc:—and also the effects of such sociological reforms on Pavlovian conditions of all children from birth and before birth, universal peace, security and stability.

The shift to the openly didactic novel had been presaged by the shift in direction of Huxley's essays. The experience of India and the influence of Lawrence had between them awakened a dormant sense of social responsibility, and from now to the end of his life Huxley was to remain concerned with the fundamental social issues of peace and freedom and the preservation of the environment; even after his conversion to mystical religion he did not retreat out of social responsibility, as many self-styled mystics have done, but remained—even if he did not long continue a political activist—intensely concerned with the plight of man in his temporal existence.

Music at Night, the volume of essays which in 1931 followed the vitalist manifesto of *Do What You Will*, can be read with particular profit as a kind of notebook for *Brave New World*. It discusses a whole series of possibilities which Huxley sees as latent in the European-American world of the late 1920s, and which will form part of the fabric of *Brave New World*: the cult of perpetual youth, the problem of leisure, the perils of Fordism to the human psyche, the possible development of eugenics as a means of shaping the man of the future, the implications of the attempt to make man primarily a consumer, and the perils to freedom of a dogmatic egalitarianism. A reading of the relevant essays shows that, though *Brave New World* is projected on to the screen of the future, it is derived almost entirely from tendencies which Huxley observed with alarm and distrust in the world around him.

Music at Night is less definite in its expression than *Brave New World*, for Huxley often presents his possibilities neutrally, with the suggestion that men in the future may use them either for good or for ill. This is the case in his discussion of the ideal drug, which in his essay, 'Wanted, a New Pleasure', he presents as a possible benefit to mankind. He suggests endowing a band of research workers to find 'the ideal intoxicant.'

> If we could sniff or swallow something that would, for five or six hours each day, abolish our solitude as individuals, atone us with our fellows in a glowing exaltation of affection and make life in all its aspects seem not only worth living, but divinely beautiful and significant, and if this heavenly, world-transfiguring drug were of such a kind that we could wake up next morning with a clear head and an undamaged constitution—then, it seems to me, all our problems (and not merely the one small problem of discovering a novel pleasure) would be wholly solved and earth become paradise.

This ideal drug will be used both negatively and positively in Huxley's novels; in *Brave New World* it provides a conditioning technique and its effect is therefore negative and life-constricting, but in *Island* (written in 1962 after Huxley had experimented with LSD) it is used in a positive Utopia as part of a technique of mental liberation.

Music at Night includes several essays which develop a theory of literature that reflects Huxley's changing practice. In 'Tragedy and the Whole Truth' he draws the opposition between two types of literature: that which, like Shakespearian tragedy, acts quickly and intensely on our feelings by isolating the dramatic elements in life, and the Wholly Truthful literature, represented by writers like Proust and Dostoevsky and Lawrence, which is 'chemically impure' and mild in its catharsis because it is based on 'the pattern of acceptance and resignation', on taking life as it is. Huxley grants that we need both kinds of literature, but it is clear that he is most attracted to Whole Truthism. In 'Art and the obvious' he points out how high art has retreated completely from certain areas of life because popular art has vulgarized them. But these aspects of life do exist.

And since they exist, they should be faced, fought with, and reduced to artistic order. By pretending that certain things are not there, which in fact *are* there, much of the most accomplished modern art is condemning itself to incompleteness, to sterility, to premature decrepitude and death.

Vulgarity in literature lies not in the content, as Huxley points out in the essay which ends *Music at Night*, but in a pretentiousness unrelated to real life. He illustrates this with a brilliant comparison between Dostoevsky and Dickens, between the death of the child Ilusha in *The Brothers Karamazov* and the death of Little Nell. Why is the first moving and the second not? It is, Huxley suggests, because Dickens isolates in a cloud of emotion the suffering and the innocence of Nell, while Dostoevsky evokes vividly the factual details of everything that happens around Ilusha's deathbed, and so relates it constantly to 'the actual realities of human life'.

These discussions of literary form are as closely related to *Brave New World* as are the speculations regarding scientific and social developments, for they draw one's attention to one of the principal reasons why this is still the most widely read of Huxley's books. It is a fantasy of the future and a satire on the present. And in both roles it carries conviction because of the expert and convincing handling of detail to create a plausible world. It is England six hundred years ahead, and Huxley has been wise enough not to change it beyond recognition. It is the country we know and a different world, and this paradox sustains our attention.

As we have seen, *Brave New World* projects happiness as the principal goal of Utopia and equates it with non-freedom. The society of the future is a parody of Plato's republic, with a small group of World Controllers ruling five castes of subjects, divided not merely socially but biologically, since they have been conditioned to their future tasks in the bottles where they were bred. To preserve happiness, the World Controllers throw away everything that might provoke either thought or passion.

The world's stable now [says Mustapha Mond, Controller for England]. People are happy; they get what they want, and they never want what they can't get. They're well off; they're safe; they're never ill; they're not afraid of death; they're blissfully ignorant of passion and old age; they're plagued with no mothers or fathers; they've got no wives, or children, or lovers to feel strongly about; they're so conditioned that they practically can't help behaving as they ought to behave.

The most striking difference between *Brave New World* and *1984*, with which it has so often been compared, is the absence of violence and overt repression.

> In the end [says Mond] the Controllers realized that force was no good. The slower but infinitely surer methods of ectogenesis, neo-Pavlovian conditions, and hypnopaedia....

Men are so conditioned from the time the spermatozoon enters the egg in the Hatchery that there is little likelihood of their breaking into rebellion; if they do become discontented there are always drugs to waft them into the heavens of restorative illusion. Thus the Controllers are able to govern with a softly firm, hand; the police use whiffs of anaesthetic instead of truncheons, and those over-brilliant individuals who do not fit the established pattern are allowed to indulge their heretical notions in the intellectual quarantine of exile.

The daily lives of the conditioned inhabitants of the brave new world are passed in a carefully regulated pattern, of production and consumption. Since it was found that too much leisure created restlessness, scientists are discouraged from devising labour-saving inventions, and the working day is followed by gregarious pleasures so organized that elaborate machinery is required and maximum consumption is encouraged. Complete freedom of sexual behaviour plus the availability of soma, provide releases from all ordinary frustrations. The abolition of viviparous birth has made families and all other permanent attachments unnecessary; individuals have become merely cells, each occupying his special position in the carefully differentiated fabric of society.

All this would not make a novel of its own; Utopian fiction that merely describes a futuristic society is notoriously tedious. Huxley brings his to life by showing the perils of any attempt at a perfect society. The higher castes of the community, the Alphas and the Betas, cannot be closely conditioned as the worker castes, because their tasks involve intelligence and the occasional need to use judgment; and even the best conditioning is not foolproof. So we get sports like the stunted Bernard Marx who has a heretical longing for solitude, like the pneumatic Lenina Crowne who is inclined to remain a little too constant in her attachments, like Helmholtz Watson who secretly writes forbidden poems about the self instead of slogans for the state.

Bernard is already suspected of disaffection and threatened with exile to Iceland, but the crisis in the life of all these three misfits in Utopia is provoked—like crises in Huxley's own life—by a journey into unfamiliarity. Bernard takes Lenina on a trip to the reservation for primitive people in New Mexico. For Lenina the first sight of dirt and disease is traumatic, but Bernard is rewarded by the discovery of a woman from Utopia who was lost years ago and has since lived and brought up her child among the Indians. The young man—John—is not only a savage; he has also, accidentally, acquired a copy of Shakespeare which, with the mixed heathen and Christian cults of the Indians, has enriched his language and shaped his outlook. In our sense he is far more 'cultured', if not more 'civilized', than the utopians.

Bernard brings the savage back to London, where he creates a sensation by his baroque behaviour and Elizabethan speech. On Bernard and Helmholtz he has the effect of crystallizing their sense of difference from the society to which they have been bred. Lenina, who is merely a Beta Plus and therefore not so inclined to intellectual rebellion, lapses into an old-fashioned infatuation for the savage, who meanwhile has conceived a romantic attachment to her. There is an extraordinarily comic scene of crossed purposes, in which the savage declares his love in resounding Shakespearian terms, whereupon Lenina, reacting in the only way she knows, unzips her garments and advances upon him in all her pneumatic nakedness, and the savage, shouting Elizabethan curses, drives her from him.

The rebellion, slight as it is, fails. The three young men, Bernard, Helmholtz and the savage, after creating a minor riot by interrupting a distribution of soma, are brought before Mustapha Mond. There is a Peacockian interlude in which each of the four characteristically reacts to the situation, and then Bernard and Helmholtz are exiled to join those who have shown themselves unreliable in the past (the real intellectual élite of the brave new world). The savage is forbidden to join them, because Mond wants to continue the experiment of subjecting him to 'civilization'. Since he cannot go anywhere else, the savage tries to establish a hermitage in the Surrey countryside of Huxley's youth, but Utopia's equivalents of newshounds discover him, and the fervent pleasure-seekers of the brave new world, hearing that he is flogging himself like a New Mexican penitent, descend on him in their helicopters. Lenina is among them. There is a great orgy in which the savage first whips and then possesses her. The next day, revolted by Utopia and his surrender to its seductions, he hangs himself.

In thematic terms, *Brave New World* opposes the scientific-industrialist ideal of Mustapha Mond (and, by derivation, of Henry Ford) to the primitivist vitalism of Lawrence, the acceptance of life with all its joys and miseries, as it exists. A decade later Huxley criticized himself for having failed to add a third possibility, that of the decentralized, libertarian society, where industry is minimized and man is liberated to pursue the life of time by the illumination of eternity. Yet it is difficult to see how the novel could have been changed to include this third possibility. The anti-individualist tendencies latent in our society have to be opposed by the poetic primitivism of the savage, who alone, since he is the only character conscious of the nature of tragedy, can embody the tragic possibilities of man's future.

One is tempted to consider *Brave New World*, because it is a Utopian fantasy, as an exceptional work that stands outside the general pattern of Aldous Huxley's fiction. In reality, its function is to close the sequence of the earlier novels. The central characters belong clearly in the Huxleian succession. Bernard is a latter-day Gumbril who has to inflate himself perpetually in order to feel equal to others, and who can only fulfil himself in exceptional circumstances. Helmholtz is a Calamy, an expert amorist who has lost his taste for sensual delights and longs for something more elevated and intelligent. The savage is a more acceptable vehicle, for the Lawrencian viewpoint than the excessively didactic Rampion. And Mustapha Mond, with his orotund delivery, is a Scogan or a Cardan who has at last made good. As for the world of the novel, it is the Bohemia of *Antic Hay* and *Point Counter Point*, carried to its logical end, its pleasures sanctified and its personal irresponsibilities institutionalized so that the freedom of the libertine is revealed as the most insidious of slaveries. There can be no doubt of the continuity between *Brave New World* and the earlier novels. It is the direction of the journey that has changed.

NOTE

[1] Shortly after publishing 'Chawdron', Huxley was to write a play, *The World of Light* (published in 1931 and produced in 1933), which concerns another aspect of possession, the phenomenon commonly described as spiritualism. Like Henry James, William Godwin, Charles Lamb and other writers who should have known better, Huxley had a persistent illusion that he was a good playwright, but *The World of Light*, like his other works for the theatre, is a very mediocre piece of writing, and is of lingering interest only because, while the pretensions of the medium in the play to communicate with the dead are proved to be false, it is later shown that he did make true revelations through his powers of telepathy. In later years the interest in parapsychology was to become an important part of Huxley's general philosophic approach.

PHILIP THODY

Brave New World

One of the many resemblances between Aldous Huxley and his grandfather lies in the interest which both men took in the question of human fertility. For Thomas Henry, it seems—rather surprisingly—to have been a personal problem as well as a concern natural in a biologist, for in 1858 he wrote to his friend Dr. Dyster that he wished 'a revised version of the Genus Homo would come out, at any rate as far as the female part of it is concerned—one half of them seem to me doomed to incessant misery so long as they are capable of childbirth'. Unlike T. H. Huxley, who eventually fathered six children, Aldous had only one son, and his concern with the problem was of a more general nature. It nevertheless recurs with obsessive force in almost all his books, and it is remarkable how early he appreciated the gravity of what is now mankind's gravest problem. In 1925 he was already commenting that any of his grandchildren who wanted to 'get away from it all' would have to take their holidays in Central Asia, and in 1956 he expressed the same idea in dramatically statistical terms when he wrote in an essay entitled *The Desert*, that 'solitude is receding at the rate of four and a half kilometres per annum'. Long before ecology, conservation and environmental studies had become fashionable concerns, he made Lord Edward Tantamount in *Point Counter Point*, speak of the 'natural, cosmic revolution' which would make man bankrupt if he continued to plunder the

From *Huxley: A Biographical Introduction.* © 1973 by Philip Thody.

planet, and in *Do What You Will* he goes so far as to argue that mankind has already passed the point of no return. Since the productivity of the machine has permitted the creation of twice the number of people than can be supported by a return of the primitive agricultural methods advocated by Gandhi, the purest idealism could have the most disastrous consequences. Tamberlaine's butcheries would be 'insignificant indeed compared with the massacres so earnestly advocated by our mild and graminivorous Mahatma', and the combination between natural fertility and human ingenuity has sprung a trap more devilish than disease itself.

It is this concern over the fact that there are now too many people for civilization to remain human that provides the first of the many strands transforming *Brave New World* into something deeper than a purely satirical account of the dehumanizing effect which science, in 1932, seemed likely to have on society. In creating a culture where human growth is deliberately stunted in the embryo in order that 'ninety-six identical twins' can work 'ninety-six identical machines', the science of *Brave New World* has merely responded to a problem created by the Ford whom Huxley found he so much admired when faced with the teeming poverty of India. Babies who come out of test-tubes naturally do so in exactly the numbers, size and type required to keep society stable, and Huxley's picture of a world wholly under human control appears at first sight to be the success story of all time. It is only on reflection that one realizes that the problems of human society have been solved in *Brave New World* in the only way that so deeply pessimistic a thinker as Huxley can really envisage: by the removal from human life of those qualities which make man different from the animals. Nobody is allowed to have children of their own, and the words 'mother' and 'father' have become the ultimate in unmentionable obscenity. People are indeed prevented from 'breeding themselves into subhuman misery'. But at the same time, they are refused any opportunity to plan their own lives, educate their own children, possess or transmit their own property, change their role, rank or employment in society, or even live permanently with another person of their own choice. Both physical and mental unhappiness have disappeared. But so too have art, religion, freedom, philosophy and poetry. The risks inseparable from man's ability to breed, to fight, to think up new ways of organizing his society, of persecuting his fellows or blowing himself to pieces, the dangers inherent in life as it naturally exists on a biological level or as man has made it through his invention of society, have been judged too great. 'Anything for a quiet life' is the basic and consciously formulated slogan of this society in which the idea of 'repressive tolerance' is put into practice with quite remarkable success. People are not only bred and conditioned to love their slavery. Any public expression of discontent is quietly put down by a police force which vaporizes the rioters with a 'euphoric, narcotic, pleasantly hallucinant' drug called soma.

There are, nevertheless, some important differences between Huxley's picture of the affluent society and the views which Herbert Marcuse and others were to put forward some thirty years after the publication of *Brave New World*. Whereas the theoreticians of the new left invariably presuppose, in their denunciation of a consumer-orientated society, that freedom and equality have been deliberately destroyed by some kind of nefarious conspiracy on the part of international capitalism and the share-holders of Marks and Spencers, Huxley's critique has no political overtones. It is the impersonal pressure of population and industry, it is man's success in his most laudable activities of eliminating disease and relieving poverty—making two blades of grass grow where only one grew before—that have made him put himself in this inhuman situation. *Brave New World* is unique in Huxley's work by its complete lack of moral indignation and its absolute ethical neutrality. Nobody is to blame, and there are no villains. Moreover, when one looks at the picture of human experience presented in Huxley's other novels, as well as in historical works such as *Grey Eminence* or *The Devils of Loudun*, the arguments put forward in defence of this benevolently administered world seem neither wholly ironic nor totally unconvincing.

It is indeed in its relationship with Huxley's work and his general personality that much of the peculiar excellence and particular fascination of *Brave New World* are to be found. Its individual themes, of course, are not new. They are announced at various points in the early novels, had been developed by other thinkers in the immediate post-war period, and are in many cases more consistent with the avowedly satirical nature of the work than with its ambiguous portrait of how human beings solve their problems by ceasing to be human. Mr Scogan, in *Crome Yellow*, evokes a future in which 'an impersonal generation will take the place of Nature's hideous system'. 'In vast state incubators', he continues, 'rows upon rows of gravid bottles will supply the world with the population it requires. The family system will disappear; society, sapped at its very base, will have to find new foundations; and Eros, beautifully and irresponsibly free, will flit like a gay butterfly from flower to flower through a sunlit world', and every one of his predictions is made to come true in *Brave New World*. Francis Chellifer, in *Those Barren Leaves*, arguing that stability can be achieved only in a society where the ideal working man is 'eight times as strong as the present day workman, with only a sixteenth of his mental capacity', defends the use of what Huxley later calls dysgenics to avoid the problems of natural intelligence, and thus anticipates the rigid caste system created in A.F. 632. The portrait in *Brave New World* of a society wholly dominated by applied science had also been anticipated outside Huxley's own work by Bertrand Russell, one of the models for Mr Scogan, in a book he had published in 1931 entitled *The Scientific Outlook*. Like Huxley, Russell had insisted on the incompatibility between a rationally organized society and any form of art or literature, and argued that the general public would, in such a society, be forbidden access to works like *Hamlet* and *Othello* 'on the grounds that they glorify private murder'. He had also observed how Pavlov's experiments could be extended to create conditioned reflexes in human beings, and the character-training in Huxley's brave new world mirrors Russell's diagnosis of how behaviourism could prevent 'lower-caste people wasting the Community's time on books'. The first sight which the Deltas have of print and pictures is accompanied by violent noises and a mild electric shock, and just as Pavlov, by consistently ringing a bell every time he gave the dog its dinner, managed to make the animal salivate by the bell alone, so the administrators in *Brave New World* ensure that the vulnerability of the human mind can be put to some practical purpose. Indeed, so much of *Brave New World* resembles *The Scientific Outlook* that one wonders at times if Huxley put any original ideas into his book.

This charge of plagiarism, however, does not apply either to Huxley's knowledge of science or to the relationship between *Brave New World* and the deeper levels of his personality. In 1963, writing in the *Memorial Volume* which he edited after his brother's death, Sir Julian Huxley went out of his way to discount rumours that Aldous's knowledge of biology always came to him at second hand. 'Most people seem to imagine', he wrote, 'that Aldous came to me for help over the biological facts and ideas he utilized so brilliantly in *Brave New World* and elsewhere in his novels and essays. This was not so. He picked them all up from his miscellaneous reading and from occasional, discussions with me and a few other biologists, from which we profited as much as he.' Moreover, what one might call the main philosophical theme in *Brave New World* is a very personal element in the novel, and its emotional impact stems from the fact that Huxley, perhaps without fully realizing what he was doing, made use of the apparently impersonal *genre* of a science fiction fantasy to express a deeply felt personal dilemma. 'A world in which ideas did not exist would be a happy world', he wrote in 1954 in his preface to Krishnamurti's *The First and Last Freedom*, and the remark is strikingly similar to the views which the Director of Hatcheries and Conditioning puts forward in the opening chapter of *Brave New World*: 'Particulars, as everyone knows, make for virtue and happiness; generalities are intellectually necessary evils. Not philosophers, but fret-sawyers and stamp collectors compose the backbone of society. The dilemma with which Mustapha Mond confronts the Savage when he has to justify the absence from the brave new world of Shakespeare, the Bible, all imaginative literature and all disinterested scientific inquiry is a real one, and the answer proposed in *Brave New World* loses its irony when placed in the context both of Huxley's early work and of his later, mystical development. Since only unhappy people produce literature, and unhappiness itself is so intense, certain and widespread, might it not be a good idea to accept that literature will disappear if suffering is abolished? Since human life requires such misery if the specifically human activities of art and science are to continue, might it not be preferable to end the requirement whereby man must live an animal existence on human terms? Why not, by removing the human element, move him nearer to the animals, and thus destroy the unhappiness which has so far been the unjustifiably high price which he has had to pay for being human?

This kind of question is one which literature normally asks. Not only is it too naïve, but the problem of inserting it into a convincing account of how people actually behave is quite insuperable. In *Point Counter Point*, for example, as in *Les Chemins de la Liberté*, *The Brothers Karamazov* or *Last Exit to Brooklyn*, the very suggestion that people could be happy if they tried is as ridiculous as the idea that they might all suddenly levitate or start to play cricket. The suggestion could only be seriously developed in a work benefiting from the science fiction convention that all things logically possible are also technically feasible. Huxley's exploitation of science fiction as a medium for the expression of ideas provides, in this respect, perhaps the final step in the acquisition for this *genre* of its literary *lettres de noblesse*. It was not only for its concision, social relevance, dramatic qualities, scientific ingenuity and technical expertise that *Brave New World* deserved the signal honour of bridging the two cultures gap by receiving an enthusiastic review from Joseph Needham in F. R. Leavis's *Scrutiny* while at the same time being described as 'a very great book' by Charlotte Haldane in *Nature*. Huxley had also, in his shortest novel since *Crome Yellow*, cast the personal dilemma which runs through his whole work into the highly general medium of a novel about the future. What he asked, over and above the question about the incompatibility between art and happiness, was whether human life could be lived on human terms, or whether the biological accident which gave man his unique status as a suffering, thinking and imaginative being should in some way be rectified. 'So you claim', remarks the World Controller when the Savage insists on contracting out of the 'brave new world' of which he has heard so much, 'the right to grow old and impotent; the right to have syphilis, and cancer; the right to have too little to eat; the right to be lousy;

the right to live in constant apprehension of what may happen tomorrow; the right to catch typhoid; the right to be tortured by unspeakable pains of every kind?' When the Savage takes a deep breath and says 'I do', the World Controller's ironic 'You're welcome to it' seems to be Huxley's own comment on such obvious lunacy.

It is true that there were, in *Nature* rather than in *Scrutiny*, doubts as to whether the question was altogether fairly put, and whether the complex emotional impulses inspiring *Brave New World* did not spoil what ought to have been an objective analysis of social and scientific problems. Thus Mrs Haldane did not limit herself to anticipating the pill and querying the degree of prescience which Huxley had shown in equipping his young ladies with 'so primitive a garment as a Malthusian belt stuffed with contraceptives when a periodic injection of suitable hormones would afford ample protection'. She also commented, in terms which her husband later regarded as revenge for the satirical portrait given of him under the character of Shearwater in *Antic Hay*, upon the dual personality which, in her view, spoilt the balance in all Huxley's novels. 'Dr. Jekyll and Mr. Hyde', she wrote, 'are nothing to Dr. Huxley and Mr. Arnold. Mr. Arnold is always doing it. He did it in *Point Counter Point*; he does it in *Brave New World*. Dr. Huxley, who knows and cares about biology and music, science and art, is again ousted by this double of his, this morbid, masochistic, medieval Christian,' and she saw the ending of the novel, in which the Savage commits suicide, as exemplifying the triumph of the Arnold over the Huxley spirit. Yet the Huxleys were no less afflicted than the Arnolds with the metaphysical concerns which Mrs Haldane clearly regarded as the function of science to dispel, and Joseph Needham went so far as to argue that it was precisely Huxley's awareness of how limited the purely scientific attitude could be which made the book so uniquely valuable. What gave the biologist a 'sardonic smile as he reads it', he declared in his review of *Brave New World* in *Scrutiny*, 'is the fact that he knows that *the biology is perfectly right*'. 'Successful experiments are even now being made', he continued, 'in the cultivation of embryos of small mammals *in vitro*, and one of the most horrible of Mr. Huxley's predictions, the production of low-grade workers of precisely identical genetic constitution from one egg, is perfectly possible. Moreover, he continued, Huxley's novel was invaluable as a description of the kind of society likely to be produced by scientists blind to any values whose existence could not be proved by laboratory experiment. It was, in short, an object lesson for the logical positivists who followed the early Wittgenstein in rejecting statements about ethics, aesthetics and religion as 'meaningless', and a particular warning to scientists of what might happen to them as well as to other people if their more enthusiastic disciples won.

This denunciation of the effect which scientific intolerance could have on society is undoubtedly one of the more conscious and deliberate aspects of *Brave New World*. When Huxley made Francis Chellifer, in *Those Barren Leaves*, remark that his father's Wordsworthian statements about nature were as meaningless as so many hiccoughs', he was already treating the cruder interpretations of the *Tractatus Logico-Philosophicus* in a half satirical light, and there is no ambiguity whatsoever about Huxley's later defence of art and literature against the new philistinism of applied science. The same is true of his attack on Freudianism, and here again the themes of *Brave New World* can be traced back to his earlier novels and short stories. Thus in *The Farcical History of Richard Greenow*, the friend who tries to psychoanalyse Richard by the free association technique favoured by the earlier Freudians receives the answer 'bosom' in response to the stimulus 'aunt' (Richard remembers playing with toy soldiers while sitting on his aunt's lap) and that of 'Wilkinson' in response to the stimulus 'God' (there floats into Richard's inward eye 'the face of a boy he had known at school and at Oxford, one Godfrey Wilkinson, called God for short'). The amateur analyst consequently infers that Richard's troubles lie in the fact that he 'had had, as a child, a great Freudian passion for his aunt; and that later on, he had had another passion, almost religious in its fervour, for someone called Wilkinson', and his complete failure to understand what is really happening to his friend foreshadows the criticism that Huxley made much later on, in 1963, in an essay called *Human Potentialities*. There, he wrote of Freud as the man 'who never mentioned any part of the human body except the mouth, the anus and the urethra', and his basic objection really changed little in the forty years separating *The Farcical History* from *Human Potentialities*. The Freudians are wrong because they take into account only one aspect of human physiology, and base their conclusions upon only one kind of evidence: that which emanates from the supposed working of the unconscious in a primarily sexual context. In *Brave New World* it is more the implied ethical teachings of Freudianism that attract his scorn, the rejection of complex and mature emotions in favour of instant gratification and the pleasure principle. His disapproval is, in fact, almost Victorian in its moral intensity, thus revealing yet another apparently contradictory strand in the complex personality of a writer whose work was regarded by *The Times*, in 1963, as having been 'devoted in the main to the violent demolition of Victorian and Edwardian values'.

Thus in *Brave New World* it is the declared aim of the authorities to translate into the sexual behaviour of adults the total irresponsibility and immaturity which supposedly characterize a child's attitude to its own body. 'When the individual feels, the community reels' is the slogan which explains why promiscuous sex is so actively encouraged, and Huxley's insistence upon this theme was another aspect of the novel which, while boosting its sales and encouraging the Australian authorities to act as his publicity agents by banning the book, attracted praise from Joseph Needham, who wrote in *Scrutiny*,

> Whether consciously or not Mr. Huxley has incorporated the views of many psychologists, e.g. Dr. Money Kryle. In an extremely interesting paper Dr. Kryle has suggested that social discontent, which has always been the driving force in social change, is a manifestation of the Oedipus complex of the members of society, and cannot be removed by economic means. With decrease of sexual taboos, these psychologists suggest, there would be a decrease in frustration and hence of that aggression which finds its outlet in religion, socialism or the more violent forms of demand for social change.

Huxley did not, in fact, need to get this idea from Dr Kryle. One of the principal themes in his own early novels is that it is much better to make love than war, and much less harmless to be a lecher than an idealist. The critical presentation of sexuality in *Brave New World* is consequently more of an indication of the general direction which his own ideas were taking than the sign of yet another intellectual debt, and his next two major works, *Eyeless in Gaza* and *Ends and Means*, mark a revulsion both against sexuality and against the total rejection of all conventional values which had characterized the early novels. The founder of the civilization described in *Brave New World* always chose to call himself, 'whenever he spoke of psychological matters, "our Freud" rather than "our Ford"', and it is doubtless as a tribute to the attitude he thus epitomized that all opportunities are taken to prevent emotional tensions building up to the point where they threaten the stability of society. The family, together with all its attendant conflicts, has been replaced by the breeding bottle and the state nursery. At the same time, the universal availability of contraceptives, together with the inculcation, in early childhood, of the duty to be promiscuous, has fulfilled Miss Triplow's prediction in *Those Barren Leaves* and 'made chastity superfluous'. All the adult emotions traditionally associated with sex—love, fidelity, a sense of responsibility, the recognition of another person as supremely and uniquely valuable—have been abolished. All that remains is a search for purely physical pleasure, with T. S. Eliot's 'pneumatic' providing the only adjective of commendation available to describe a woman's charms. If the contraceptives should fail to work, the flood-lit abortion centre in Chelsea provides a ready alternative; and the 'Pregnancy advisory centres' so liberally advertised in the London of 1972 provide yet another example of how some of Huxley's prophecies are being fulfilled more quickly than he expected.

The Freudian idea that we should avoid repressions and frustrations, that the way to happiness lies in the satisfaction of those primitive, instinctual, sexual drives which previous societies have been compelled to inhibit, is thus criticized first and foremost for the effect that it has on people's emotional life. Although he does not specifically mention it, one of the 'established spiritual values' whose importance Huxley rediscovered at the end of *Jesting Pilate* was a belief in monogamy and what one is almost tempted to call romantic love. In *Brave New World* Bernard Marx would like to spend the day alone with his loved one Lenina, walking by themselves in the Lake District, and this almost Wordsworthian attitude to nature, presented in *Those Barren Leaves* in an essentially comical light, is another sign of how Huxley's attitudes were changing. In *Brave New World*, however, the constant reduction of adult human beings to childlike animals is also associated with the deliberate destruction of all intellectual curiosity, and it is difficult to tell whether it is the stunting of the emotions or the prostitution of the mind which Huxley finds most abhorrent. In 'After Ford (or Freud) 632', the only criteria by which society judges itself are those of stability and efficiency. Free, disinterested, open-ended research is consequently regarded as being just as dangerous as art, literature or religion, for the essential characteristic of true scientific inquiry is that no one can know whither it might lead. Each member of society is permitted to know only so much as is immediately relevant to the tasks he has to perform, and even those alpha-plus intellectuals whose pre- and post-natal conditioning has left them with enough intelligence to think for themselves are not allowed to explore any new ideas.

Huxley's realization that the systematic application of technology could lead to a situation where science itself is considered highly dangerous is yet another indication of the fundamental similarity between his attitudes and those of his grandfather. If there was anything to which Thomas Henry Huxley unremittingly devoted his enormous energy, it was the propagation to all members of society of the methods and ideals of scientific inquiry. It was consequently as much by respect for family tradition as through personal taste that Aldous Huxley made this destruction of science by its own hand into an important theme in the actual plot of *Brave New World*, and in this he was quite consciously using a novel about the future to comment on current development in his and our society. The plot revolves round the discovery, by Bernard Marx and Lenina Crowne, of the existence in one of the 'savage reservations' in South America, of Linda, a woman from their own civilization who had been lost some twenty years earlier during an outing very similar to their own. By an unfortunate and almost incredible accident, Linda's excursion among the Pueblo Indians had coincided with her getting pregnant by her lover—now Director of World Hatcheries. By an ironic reversal of traditional standards, it is the very fact that she has had a baby which has prevented her from appealing to her own civilization for help, and she has been forced to bring up her son alone. When he had asked questions—'How did the world begin?', 'What are chemicals?'—Linda had been totally unable to reply. The only book she had ever heard of was her own work manual on *The Chemical and Bacteriological Conditioning of the Embryo: Practical Instructions for Beta Workers* and all she knew of chemicals was that they came out of bottles. It is by the quality of the human beings it produces that a civilization can be judged, and it is in the character of Linda that we see what the inhabitants of *Brave New World* are really like and what our own culture might become if the pressures for wholly vocational education are allowed to triumph. They have lost all their adaptability, all their ability and willingness to understand other people, all sense of wonder and curiosity, and all power to withstand, in loneliness and isolation, the human experiences of being persecuted or facing death. In his early novels, Huxley seemed to many critics to have followed his grandfather's iconoclastic example and destroyed any Victorian values still left standing after Thomas Henry had so convincingly demolished their religious foundations. In *Brave New World* it is not only the implied insistence on the importance of marriage and pre-marital chastity which suggests that he is going back to what was best in both the agnostic and the Protestant traditions of Victorian England. Education, he implies, must involve more than a vigorous intellectual training in the arts and sciences. Children must also learn to bear misfortune with courage, and to postpone their pleasures until they can face up to their responsibilities. Sexual permissiveness, intellectual conformism and social stability may perhaps lead to a more efficient and comfortable society than has ever existed in the past. But on no account must they be preferred to the ideals of responsibility and self-reliance which have so far characterized the essentially Protestant tradition of Western democracy.

Matthew and even Thomas Arnold would, in this respect, have felt just as much sympathy as Thomas Henry Huxley for the character depicted with most approval in *Brave New World*. Helmholtz Watson, whose lectures on Advanced Emotional Engineering are much admired both by his students and the Authorities, decides to opt out of the comfortable world of an alpha-plus literary intellectual and chooses instead to undergo the rigours of life on an isolated island. There, he will at least have the opportunity of thinking his own thoughts, even though the fact that he does so in conditions of intellectual quarantine will effectively prevent him from influencing what goes on elsewhere. What is equally significant, however, is that the character who more convincingly represents Huxley himself, Bernard Marx, finally lacks the strength of character needed to support loneliness and exile. Like Philip Quarles, Bernard Marx is an alpha-plus intellectual with a physical defect. The rumour runs that 'somebody made a mistake when he was still in the bottle—thought he was a gamma and put alcohol into his blood surrogate', and Bernard consequently suffers from the same feelings of personal inadequacy which characterize all Huxley's autobiographical figures. By tastes and instinct, he resembles the inner-directed man of the Protestant tradition. Yet because of his physical defect, he lacks the psychological qualities which would enable him to fight successfully against the outer-directed, managerial society in which he lives. The self-confidence emanating from the public careers of the earlier generation of Arnolds and Huxleys has disappeared. What takes its place, in *Brave New World*, is not only a fuller realization of how physiological accidents can destroy moral stamina. There is also a more disturbing awareness of how ambiguous certain kinds of moral behaviour can be, and of how preferable an attitude of critical detachment might consequently become. It is never long, in *Brave New World*, before what appears to be a straightforward attack on contemporary trends takes on more ambiguous overtones and what W. H. G. Armytage, in *Yesterday's Tomorrows*, classifies as the product of a 'disenchanted mechanophobe' reveals more disturbing if more interesting implications.

In the eighteenth century, and especially in the *Contes* of Voltaire or Diderot, the role of the outsider in fiction was fairly easily defined. It was to provide, by the introduction of the common sense supposedly prevailing elsewhere, a criticism of the nonsensical principles on which modern, European civilization was based. There is also an outsider in *Brave New World*, Linda's son John, who is rescued from the savage reservation and brought to London by Bernard Marx, and it is his reactions to the marvellous world which he has heard about from his mother which provide the main story line in the novel. By a happy accident, his reading has not been limited to *The Chemical and Bacteriological Conditioning of the Embryo: Practical Instructions for Beta Workers*. He has also read one of the forbidden works of AF 632, *The Complete Works of William Shakespeare*, and it is by the standards of Shakespearian tragedy and romance that he judges the society which finds him so delicious and stimulating a novelty. Lenina Crowne seems to him the most beautiful and perfect creature he has ever seen, and he falls madly and devotedly in love with her. But instead of going to bed with her straight away as the other young men of her acquaintance have all been conditioned to do in such circumstances, the Savage behaves very oddly. He insists on her fitting in not only with *Romeo and Juliette* but with the even more extraordinary concepts he has absorbed from the fertility rites and initiation ceremonies of the Pueblo Indians. When she cannot understand what he is talking about—and she is quite incapable of imagining that anyone else's frame of reference could possibly be different from hers—John seeks refuge in an isolated and abandoned air-lighthouse on the Hog's Back. There, revolted by the spectacle of a society from which all effort, skill, sympathy and patience have been removed, he tries to go back to nature and live by his own efforts. Less rationally, he also tries to whip his body into an acceptance of the chastity which the memories of Lenina's charms make into an impossible ideal, but in AF 632, any deviation from the norm, and especially one with such intriguing sexual overtones, attracts crowds of spectators. Lenina is among them, and tries to come and talk to John. But the Savage, already 'frantically, without knowing it', wishing that the blows he is giving his own body were raining down on Lenina, strikes at her with his whip. She stumbles and falls, and as he strikes again and again 'at his own rebellious flesh, or at that plump incarnation of turpitude writhing in the heather at his feet', events get out of hand in a way that gives Huxley's attempt to revive the moral values of nineteenth-century England some disquieting overtones. The crowd of spectators 'drawn by the fascination of the horror of pain and, from within, impelled by that habit of cooperation, that desire for unanimity and atonement, which their conditioning had so ineradicably implanted in them', begin to imitate his gestures. Soon, John's search for purity has turned into a sado-masochistic orgy; and the outsider who, in an age more certain of its values, would have represented triumphant sanity, hangs himself in despair.

Another possible if less dramatic sign of the ambiguous attitude which Huxley encourages his reader to adopt towards the society described in *Brave New World* is the extremely humane provision made for those who wish to explore heterodox ideas. When Helmholtz Watson goes off to think his own thoughts, write his own books and perhaps even invent his own God, no one will be allowed to interfere with him. He will, to use Isaiah Berlin's distinction in *Two Concepts of Liberty*, be endowed with all the negative freedom that a man can desire. What he will not have, however, is what Isaiah Berlin calls positive freedom: the opportunity to try to impose his own will on the outside world. The 'repressive tolerance' of consumer orientated society is indeed fully consistent both with certain forms of intellectual freedom and with the behaviour of those individuals who feel that their first duty is towards themselves. What it does not and cannot allow is any changes in its own fundamental patterns. Huxley seems almost to be recommending the *Brave New World* solution as the correct one when he writes, in the opening chapter of *The Perennial Philosophy*, of the way in which 'provision was and still is made by every civilized society for giving thinkers a measure of protection from the ordinary stresses and strains of social life. The hermitage, the monastery, the college, the academy and the research laboratory; the begging bowl, the endowment, the patronage, and the grant of tax-payers' money—such are the principal devices that have been used by actives to conserve that rare bird, the religious, philosophical or scientific contemplative.' Whereas Thomas Henry Huxley—like his other grandson Julian—was a man of action as well as an intellectual, a teacher and administrator as well as an author who helped to change man's concept of his nature, Aldous Huxley limited himself for most of his life to sitting in a room and writing books. Each of the devices he mentions in *The Perennial Philosophy* is characterized by the assumption that the thinker will be neither expected nor allowed to emerge from his ivory tower and play a role in the society that subsidizes his production of ideas, and the islands to which the authorities of *Brave New World* exile their deviant intellectuals would have suited Huxley down to the ground. It was nevertheless in the years immediately following the publication of what still remains his most successful work that Huxley ceased to be what he himself later described as an 'amused, Pyrrhonic aesthete' who stood aside from the world and laughed. For all their gloom and violence, the thirties were still to some extent a time of hope, and the very acuteness of the crisis through which Western society was passing created a future that still seemed to be relatively open. Huxley was one of the many intellectuals and writers who then tried to play an active part in politics and avoid the horrors which, for those who read it in the forties, made *Brave New World* seem even more like a paradise.

ROBERT S. BAKER

Brave New World: *Huxley's Dystopian Dilemma*

T he world of the seventh century after Ford is a projection of Huxley's increasingly somber assessment of the course of modern history—an alternative world systematically conceived as an anti-utopia or, more precisely, a dystopia in which the course of history has been diverted to apparently rational ends. While drawing on many of the traditional utopian conventions, the literary ancestry of *Brave New World* can be traced back to the evolutionary romance, an Edwardian genre for the most part played out by 1914. H. Robert Huntley has characterized the Darwinian controversy insofar as it affected this genre in the late Victorian and Edwardian periods as one "that implanted the notion of 'process' indelibly on the Western mind, while leaving it free to interpret the end of that process as either promise or threat for the well-being of mankind." The distant evolutionary good of the greatest number, or in Huxley's terms the "Higher Utilitarianism" of Mustapha Mond's World State, was a recurrent theme in novels like Bulwer-Lytton's *The Coming Race* (1871), W. H. Hudson's *A Crystal Age* (1887), or the various evolutionary romances of H. G. Wells. *Brave New World* can be described as a literary descendent of the evolutionary romance to the extent that it analyzes the behavior of a future race in the context of radically evolved biological types; but in this later variant of the genre, the arbitrary and unpredictable processes of natural selection have been supplanted and

From *The Dark Historic Page: Social Satire and Historicism in the Novels of Aldous Huxley 1921 – 1939.* © 1982 by The University of Wisconsin Press.

rationalized by eugenics. The striking opening scene in the Central London Hatchery is a satirical tableau in which the Fordean production line merges with the scientific laboratory where Mond's apprentice sorcerers concoct, nurture, and decant a witch's brew of artificially evolved types. But if evolution has been brought under the control of social engineering and eugenics, history too has been nullified by the scientists and technicians of the "World State," where both "historicism" and "developmentalism" have become archaic concepts bereft of any trace of meaning.

Throughout the twenties Huxley repeatedly expressed his misgivings concerning not only the methodological principles underlying the study of the past but the actual course taken by modern British and European history. By 1928 he had become increasingly aware of the threat posed by the two principal variants of modern totalitarianism, Italian fascism and Russian communism. While neither as overtly political nor as sensitive to contemporary developments in Europe as *Eyeless in Gaza* or *After Many a Summer Dies the Swan*, *Brave New World* is an implicit condemnation of collectivist absolutism, despite the fact that in Huxley's dystopia, coercion is exercised in an ingratiatingly mild and benevolent form. The inhabitants of the World State are condemned to a life of discreetly stimulated apathy, and as Huxley argued in a letter to George Orwell, he firmly believed that his gently paternalistic form of despotism was much more likely to evolve out of current historical conditions than the systematically violent alternative envisaged in *Nineteen Eighty-Four*. Of equal significance, however, the autocratic utilitarians governing the World State have succeeded in solving the problem of the meaning and direction of history that had exercised Huxley throughout the 1920s; they have simply banished it by fiat.

In *Ends and Means*, published five years after *Brave New World*, Huxley speculated on the path of "regression" taken by modern history, contrasting it to a conceivably "non-Euclidean history" with its potentially utopian line of development: "it would be interesting to construct a historical 'Uchronia' (to use Renouvier's useful word), based upon the postulate that Robespierre and the other Jacobin leaders were convinced pacifists. The 'non-Euclidean' history deducible from this first principle would be a history, I suspect, innocent of Napolean, of Bismarck, of British imperialism and the scramble for Africa, of the World War, of militant Communism and Fascism, of Hitler and universal rearmament" (*EM*, 145). *Brave New World* is the darker antithesis of such a hopeful Uchronia, a satiric dystopia based on a rejection of current European ideology, including its ancillary belief in limitless technological innovation. And while history is denied in Huxley's Fordean society, the World State is the direct outgrowth of, in his terms, a bleakly

"Euclidean" series of historical undulations. In *The Olive Tree*, which appeared four years after *Brave New World*, Huxley speculated on the existence of collective trends shaping and informing the flow of historical events but never manifesting themselves in such a way as to be susceptible to scientific formulation.

As I observed in chapter one, Huxley's "historical undulations" are not nomological entities operating according to scientific laws but rather broad cultural tendencies, heterogenous in form and psychological in nature. Equally important, Huxley on occasion associated them with a rhythmic oscillation between alternating states of "decadence" and cultural vigor: "The history of any nation follows an undulatory course. In the trough of the wave we find more or less complete anarchy; but the crest is not more or less complete Utopia, but only, at best, a tolerably humane, partially free and fairly just society that invariably carries within itself the seeds of its own decadence" (*CE*, 277). Throughout the interwar period Huxley consistently disparaged theoretical generalizations regarding historical process, but in the essays and satirical narratives of the 1930s, he did occasionally introduce the concept of cyclical process. Moreover, his playful use of the term "Euclidean" does hint at a nomological emphasis; that is, a history proceeding according to laws and axioms systematically and logically deducible from each another. The "trough" and "crest" of Huxley's historical wave finds its antecedent in *Point Counter Point* where Rampion revised Wellsian theories of linear "progress" in terms of a pattern of "peaks and declines" (*PCP*, 291). Similarly, Mark Staithes of *Eyeless in Gaza* will employ Gibbon's *Decline and Fall* as a touchstone in his attempt to gauge the current status of British and European history. However, I believe the bleakly Spenglerian caste of Huxley's assessment of events in Europe and England is symptomatic less of a shift in his estimate of history's comprehensibility than of his despair regarding a series of events which, as he informed E. M. Forster, seemed to be moving irrevocably toward "some fantastic denial of humanity" and in a discernibly "*straight, un-dulating trajectory*" (italics mine). The "inward decay" of *Point Counter Point* had become in the thirties outright "regression" in a society where the forces of history had outstripped even Rampion's prophecies of an apocalyptic "gallop toward death" (*PCP*, 437).

In *Brave New World* Huxley attempted to envisage a very distant development of the society depicted in *Antic Hay* and *Point Counter Point*. The liberal "Utopia" of tolerable humaneness and partial freedom described in *The Olive Tree* was rejected in favor of a more likely alternative, a collectivist dystopia. Occupying neither the "crest" nor the "trough" of the wave, Mustapha Mond's World State is a massive socioeconomic improvisation marking the termination of history, an apocalyptic ushering-in of a society so authoritarian and immobile that historical process has been halted, rather like a river frozen in its bed. As an attempt to dam up the forces of history, such a society is founded on fear and revulsion, specifically a dread of those libidinal and sadomasochistic drives that Huxley had previously dramatized in the irrational urges and violent attitudes of socially emblematic characters like Maurice Spandrell, Lucy Tantamount, Everard Webley, and Illidge of *Point Counter Point*. Throughout the period 1928 to 1939, Huxley's letters and essays illustrate his belief that he could detect social processes at work that seemed vaguely and only conjecturally lawlike in their pervasive effect and apparent inevitability. This intractably "Euclidean" set of conditions he associated with social fragmentation, increasingly irrational behavior, moral "decadence," and a kind of social death-wish. In *Brave New World* Mustapha Mond's government had come into being only after a period in which these forces or tendencies (i.e. Huxley's "undulations") had been given unlimited play during the "Nine Years' War."

The World State, then, is premised on the futility of history, specifically a denial of the concept of progress and a revulsion for "the remote past" (*BNW*, 112), any mention of which is regarded as an unforgivable solecism. The inhabitants of the seventh century after Ford are "taught no history" (*BNW*, 39) in compliance with Ford's dictum that "history is bunk" (*BNW*, 38). *Brave New World*, however, is provided with a schematic past, the salient events of which emerge gradually in the course of the novel and when summarized form a sequence of events that conform to Huxley's "deteriorationist" perspective. The chronology of Fordian and pre-Fordian history begins with a period of increasing violence and widespread social instability:

A.F. 141:   Outbreak of "The Nine Years' War" followed by "the great Economic Collapse." A period of Russian ecological warfare including the poisoning of rivers and the anthrax bombing of Germany and France.

A.F. 150:   Beginning of "World Control."
                  The "conscription of consumption" followed by a period of social restiveness and instability.
                  The rise of "Conscientious objection and [a] back to nature movement."
                  The reaction to liberal protest movements.

The Golders Green massacre of "Simple Lifers."
The British Museum Massacre.
Abandonment of force by the World Controllers.
Period of an anti-history movement and social reeducation including intensive propaganda directed against viviparous reproduction as well as a "campaign against the Past." Museums closed.
Suppression of all books published before A.F. 150.

A.F. 178:   Government subsidization of special programs in pharmacology and biochemistry.
Stabilization of the World State.

A.F. 473:   The Cyprus Experiment: establishment of a wholly Alpha community.

A.F. 478:   Civil war in Cyprus.
Nineteen thousand Alphas killed.

A.F. 482 (approx.): The Ireland Experiment (increased leisure time and four-hour work week).

A.F. 632:   The present of *Brave New World*.

The achievement of, in Mustapha Mond's words, "the stablest equilibrium in history" (*BNW*, 272) is attributable to a paralysis of historical process that extends to the individual citizen in a world where birth immediately to arrested development. For Mond the clamant needs of his society, indeed the exigencies of history itself, have finally been provided for by a pantheon of cultural heroes including Henry Ford, Freud, Pavlov, Marx, and Lenin. The World State is a wholly secular culture, dominated by economics, supported by technology, and dedicated to the—within carefully set limits—Freudian pleasure principle with its emphasis on libidinal appetite. In brief, Mond's carefully controlled society involves an immersion in the present in which Pavlovian conditioning, Marxist collectivism, Fordean technology, and a calculated indulgence of Freudian infantile appetitiveness combine to rigidly stabilize society and undermine the concept of linear progress.

Cut off from the past and heedless of a future that no longer beckons with the promise of an enlargement of knowledge or a further refinement of consciousness, the inhabitants of Mond's Fordean culture no longer aspire to a good "somewhere beyond, somewhere outside the present" (*BNW*, 211). As the names of many of the characters suggest (Bernard Marx, Hubert Bakunin, Sarojini Engels, Lenina Crowne, and Polly Trotsky), the Fordean dystopia is a workers' paradise where the state, instead of withering away, has metastasized into a benevolent despotism that in a very general sense Huxley extrapolated from the secularist materialism of Marx and Lenin. The hinted connection with Marxism and Leninism is tenuous at best, but it does serve to remind the reader of Huxley's identification of Russian socialism with the new romanticism and its "disparagement of spiritual and individual values" (*MN*, 216). For Huxley "the Bolsheviks are romantic in denying that man is anything more than a social animal, susceptible of being transformed by proper training into a perfect machine." In essence this is the fundamental postulate of Mond's perverted socialism, a new romantic preoccupation with "human biology and economics" (*MN*, 215) culminating in the transformation of human beings into reliable and predictable mechanisms. To that extent *Brave New World* prophesies the ultimate triumph of the new romanticism.

Flying over the New Mexico landscape, Bernard Marx notes the presence of an electric fence demarcating the boundary between civilization and the "savagery" of the reservation: "the fence marched on and on, irresistibly the straight line, the geometrical symbol of triumphant human purpose" (*BNW*, 123). But such New Romantic linearity had reached its terminus in the World State, and despite the sleep-inculcated principle that "progress is lovely" (*BNW*, 118), no further development is contemplated by the World Controllers. Mustapha Mond firmly repudiates the notion of "scientific progress" and its corollary "that it could be allowed to go on indefinitely, regardless of everything else" (*BNW*, 273). Having reached its apotheosis in the World State, history has been displaced by a static present founded on a carefully selective approach to technology and science; as a result, progress has become a noun lacking a meaningful referent. Keith May has observed that "*Brave New World* is a portrait of a dilemma," the quandary being an ambiguous polarization between the utopian and the primitive, or "between the minimization of suffering and the positive search for suffering." In large measure this is the case, but the Savage Reservation is as much an insulated time capsule as the Fordean World State. The former is a weird agglomeration of ancient religious and barbaric customs. Thriving on supernatural rituals that in turn are founded on the presumed efficacy of suffering, the Savage Reservation is a small dystopia existing within what purports to be a larger utopian state. Carefully quarantined, it is an unnatural survival from "the Bottomless Past" (*BNW*, 116), part museum for the benefit of prudently chosen tourists, part concentration camp for those who cannot be smoothly assimilated into Mond's ideal state. But the atavistic suffering that it offers is without meaning, compounded equally of religious violence and a broad range of physical ailments, including disease, arbitrary violence, and the aging process. Admittedly, the pain that pervades the reservation does hold out the promise of rousing Bernard from the soma torpor of the World State, but it remains an unsatisfactory alternative as a consequence of its essential barbarity. Indeed, these two apparently contrasting cultures actually mirror each other in a number of ways. History is no more relevant to the inhabitants of the reservation than to the citizens of Fordean civilization. Both societies are morally coercive, while the debasing violence of the fertility ritual finds its attenuated counterpart in the repressed violence of the communal orgies of Bernard's London.

Like *Point Counter Point*, *Brave New World* achieves closure with an act of calculated yet futile rebellion followed by a sexual orgy and a suicide. Spandrell's murder of the fascist Everard Webley finds its distant echo in the climactic scene at the Park Lane Hospital, where John the Savage, spurred by the Fascist regimentation of the Delta workers, attempts to foment a social uprising. Burlap's private bathroom tryst with Beatrice is expanded at the close of *Brave New World* to an appropriately public sadomasochistic saturnalia, while the suicide of Spandrell is reenacted by John the Savage. Both suicides proceed from similarly complicated sources. As I argued earlier, Spandrell's self immolation is motivated only in part by his inability to discover meaning in the secularized and atomistic society of *Point Counter Point*; it is also, perhaps even principally, a masochistic gesture directed at his mother as a consequence of his belief that she had prostituted herself by betraying him to his rival, Major Knoyle. John the Savage is also deeply scarred by his memories of what he regards as his mother's promiscuity. Singled out by the savage community as sexually profligate, she is enshrined in his consciousness as a woman who surrendered herself to a hostile masculine interloper who literally shuts the young John out of his mother's life. The memory of "Linda and Popé" (*BNW*, 156) in bed is a trauma from which John never recovers. It is linked to his mother's whipping by the Indian women and expresses itself in his own desire to be whipped during the fertility ceremony. Both the public exposure of Linda and her beating are reenacted by John when, years later, he whips Lenina Crowne at the air-lighthouse and inadvertently provokes a mass scene of erotic flagellation. As I have argued in earlier chapters, the ideas and erotic practice of the Marquis de Sade were an important element in Huxley's philosophy of history, bracketed in his mind with what he referred to as the nihilist revolution,

cultural decadence, and a final historical period of complete moral
bankruptcy—an association of ideas that accounts for the pervasive presence
of sadism and references to de Sade throughout Huxley's satire from 1928 to
1939.

The Savage, then is a virtual avatar of Maurice Spandrell, consumed by
the same anxieties and fears, similarly obsessed with female promiscuity as
well as what he takes to be his mother's unchastity, and bent with the same
neurotic intensity upon self-destruction. The Freudian family romance,
despite Huxley's repeatedly expressed misgivings concerning Freud's
emphasis on erotic behavior, is one of the principal satirical conventions of
his social satire. *Brave New World* is no exception to this practice, and Huxley
will employ it again but in much greater detail in both *Eyeless in Gaza* and
After Many a Summer Dies the Swan. For Huxley these strangely troubled
sadomasochistic figures were satirical types (part of his "Sadean sociology")
as well as psychological studies, and in the former role were intended to
reflect the historical conditions of a gradually deteriorating society. The
Savage's suicide cannot be attributed solely to the pernicious impact of
Fordean civilization on a mind unprepared for such an onslaught. Therefore
his death significantly complicates the satirical direction of *Brave New World*,
implicating both the irrational freedom of the Reservation as well as the
oppressive regimentation of the World State.

The dilemma confronting Bernard Marx is equally ambiguous. By
introducing a young man already psychologically crippled into the libidinal
freedoms of Fordean London, Huxley deliberately skewed the satiric clarity
of *Brave New World*. Bernard Marx is a similarly compromised character. As
a self-conscious individual swallowed up in a social body numbed by drugs
and permeated by conformist categories of response, he must confront the
implications of his egocentric aspirations. No revolutionary and at best only
a moderate opponent of Mond's paternalistic despotism, he oscillates
between a despairing conformity and a servile endorsement of Fordean
values. Moreover, he never fully comprehends the nature of the choices
facing him, while the mainspring propelling much of his behavior lies with
his sense of sexual inadequacy. His aimless peregrinations in the company of
Lenina Crowne is another Huxleyan satiric convention, establishing Bernard
as a typically intimidated Huxleyan protagonist, uncertain as to his social
role, anxious regarding his relationship with women, and bemused by his
own promptings to resist the pressures of a society the intellectual or
spiritual postulates of which he can neither endorse nor reject. Like
Theodore Gumbril of *Antic Hay*, Bernard resists the demands of his
profession and yearns to realize an elusive goal of romantic monogamy, a

predilection that links him to the Savage. But his progression from social outcast to social lion corresponds to his gradual adoption of an increasingly condescending role of patron and mentor to the Savage whom he had previously discovered at the New Mexico Reservation. Unwittingly adopting the role of Mustapha Mond, he instructs his protégé in the customs of Fordean culture, only to become progressively outraged by the Savage's nonconformist objections. Similarly, his deliberate exposure of his superior at the Central London Hatchery as the father of the Savage is less an act of social rebellion than a spiteful act of personal revenge. The sequence of events following his return from the Savage Reservation, instead of leading to his gradual emancipation from the regimentation of the World State, feeds his eager insecurity, binding him closer to the values of Mustapha Mond. In short, in a manner characteristic of the social satire of the twenties, Huxley refuses to permit a significant degree of development in his major satiric protagonist. Bernard Marx fails to transcend the values and customs of Fordean society, while John the Savage—the one character whose fresh perspective is capable of reinforcing Bernard's insurgent iconoclasm—is undermined at the very outset by his psychotic response to female sexuality. John the Savage gradually displaces Bernard Marx as Huxley's principal protagonist in the latter half of the novel. Usurping the affection of Lenina Crowne and winning the friendship of Helmholtz Watson as well as the grudging respect of Mustapha Mond, the Savage's reactions to the radical simplifications of Fordean Utilitarianism seem especially designed to expose the self-contradictions of Bernard Marx's character. On the other hand, the Savage's choice of suffering and isolation is not an unalloyed good; indeed, in *Eyeless in Gaza* the choice of pain as a concomitant of individual identity is in large part denounced by Huxley as a potentially degenerate impulse. Similarly, Helmholtz Watson's choice of Promethean isolation and Shelleyan romanticism is equally unacceptable to the author of *Music at Night* and *Ends and Means.*

In their endeavor to direct the course of history to apparently rational ends, Huxley's World Controllers fostered the development of a society that cherished above all else collective stability and historical stasis. In the novel this revolutionary exercise in control over populations and economic processes had begun after the Nine Years' War, but in actual history, in Soviet Russia—although Huxley insisted that traces of the same processes could be detected in Europe, Great Britain, and North America. Huxley associated such unwelcome developments with the New Romantic fascination with technological progress, and yet the absence of suffering in Mustapha Mond's utopia is attributable to the systematic eradication of precisely those attributes of human nature that Huxley himself found most objectionable. It is this fact that accounts for the curiously ambiguous quality of Huxley's social criticism in *Brave New World*. In this respect, it can be said that Huxley has created his dystopia in order to frame a complicated question in the guise of an apparently simple juxtaposition of contending points of view. A significant number of Mustapha Mond's principal beliefs, including his repudiation of history, disavowal of the value of the individual ego, dismissal of unlimited historicist progress, rejection of art, and aversion for the family, were shared at this time by Huxley. Indeed, they form the staple subjects of his satirical fiction throughout the interwar period. Mond's political and sociological hypotheses, however, proceed from a corrupted source, one Huxley will explore in greater detail in *Eyeless in Gaza*, while Mond's neurotic quest for absolute material security will reach its psychotic apotheosis in Joseph Stoyte's castle-museum in *After Many a Summer Dies the Swan*. Most important, his consuming passion for a completely regulated society involved an assault on mind and intelligence that Huxley could never countenance.

The secular and material values of the World State represent a massive projection of Lucy Tantamount's insistence in *Point Counter Point* that in the "aeroplane" there is "no room" for "the soul" (*PCP*, 282). Just as John the Savage is a variation on Maurice Spandrell, Lenina Crowne is a damped-down version of Lucy Tantamount, shorn of the latter's neurasthenic restiveness and sadomasochistic violence. Like Lucy, Lenina is a fervent admirer of machinery, a believer in progress, and a promiscuous sensualist. To create a secure society for neurotic hedonists like Lucy Tantamount, to purge them of their libidinally destructive drives in an environment of carefully stimulated apathy, is in essence the *raison d'être* of the World State. For Huxley this was a goal of sorts, indeed the only one he could envision for the Europe of the late 1920s. As Mustapha Mond observed, "liberalism ... was dead of anthrax" (*BNW*, 57), a casualty of the Nine Years' War.

Huxley associated liberalism with the old romanticism and its stress on individuality, unlimited historical development, and political freedom. Like "history," it is a concept that has no relevance to Fordean paternalism and its monolithic embodiment in the World State. The World Controllers are not presented as charismatic leaders, nor do they require an electoral consensus in order to act. The end of history necessarily implies the death of politics in a world where the rulers have become faceless technocrats, worshipping efficiency and regulation, and administering a complex social system that has no need of ideological justification beyond sleep-taught clichés. Despite these objections to the despotic paternalism of the World Controllers,

Huxley permits Mustapha Mond to formulate in the final chapters a detailed apology for Fordean collectivism, including systematic governmental intrusion into and domination of all spheres of human existence. Mond's objections to the psychological and economic anarchy that he believes informs the entire gamut of human history are essentially Huxley's, and his collectivist materialism was if not the most desirable answer to Sadean anarchy, at least a conceivable solution. It should be stressed that the sadistic irrationality Huxley linked with the society of *Point Counter Point* was for the most part a trait of John the Savage, not Mustapha Mond; and while Huxley consistently repudiated Marxist collectivism, he nevertheless observed in a letter written in 1931, approximately two years before the appearance of *Brave New World*, that "the Marxian philosophy of life is not exclusively true: but, my word, it goes a good way, and covers a devil of a lot of ground." A month later he observed in another letter that history was an incurable disease and Marxist economics merely another symptom of social decay: "the human race fills me with a steadily growing dismay. I was staying in the Durham coal-field this autumn, in the heart of English unemployment and it was awful. If only one could believe that the remedies proposed for the awfulness (Communism etc.) weren't even worse than the disease—in fact weren't the disease itself in another form, with superficially different symptoms.

Mond of course is not a Marxist; however, his ideas are similar enough, in the broadest sense, to suggest the scope and depth of the philosophical dilemma in which Huxley found himself in the early thirties. In his next novel, *Eyeless in Gaza*, Huxley will turn to the theme of political engagement—a subject, with the exception of *Point Counter Point*, noticeably absent from the satires of the twenties. Its exigent presence in the world of Maurice Spandrell and Anthony Beavis signals Huxley's departure from the familiar terrain of Eliot's *Waste Land* and his long-postponed incursion into Auden country.

PETER EDGERLY FIRCHOW

The End of Utopia:
A Study of Aldous Huxley's Brave New World

If there are plenty of good scientific and technological reasons—ectogenesis, cloning, serial mass production, TV—why *Brave New World* could not have been written before it was, there are also some very good literary reasons. For *Brave New World* is, literarily speaking, a very modern book; modern not only because it deals frankly with a typically modern subject like sex, but modern in the very ways it conceives of and presents its subject and characters.

There are in *Brave New World* no long introductory descriptions of landscape or environment in the Victorian or Edwardian manner; there is, initially, no attempt to give more than a very rudimentary outline of the physical and psychological traits of the characters. There is no elaborate explanation of how we came to be where we are, nor even at first an explanation at all why we are where we are: six-hundred-odd years in the future. The starting assumption is simply that it is quite normal to be in a big factory in the middle of London. Only gradually and indirectly does that assumption also become startling, as it becomes clear to us what the products of this factory are and what kind of a world we have entered.

This technique of indirection is one that Virginia Woolf ascribes, in Mr. Bennett and Mrs. Brown (1924), to the moderns. For her—and by extension for the modern novelist—the way to get at the heart of a character

From *The End of Utopia: A Study of Aldous Huxley's* Brave New World. © 1984 by Bucknell University Press.

105

and a situation is not to add up every item of information we can gather about them; the whole is not to be found in the summing up of all of the parts. That way lies dullness, and Arnold Bennett. The better way is to try to get at the whole by being, as it were, paradoxically content with the part. To get at the essence of Mrs. Brown—Woolf's hypothetical example—we need to be told nothing directly of her history and background; we merely need to overhear her conversation in a railway compartment for an hour or so. Out of the apparently random odds and ends of this conversation, we can, by an act of the imagination, reconstruct her life and penetrate her soul.

What happens when a modern novelist resolves to transfer a Mrs. Brown or any other person into a work of fiction is that, inevitably, the author himself more or less disappears; the reader is left alone, seemingly at least, with the character(s). The modern novel therefore involves a shift of responsibility for character and situation away from the author and toward the reader, who must reach his conclusions about both unaided. This is clearly what happens in Virginia Woolf's own novels, or in the novels of other modern writers like Waugh, Bowen, Isherwood, and Huxley.

This is not to say that Huxley or Isherwood or anyone else read Woolf and then decided to write a new kind of novel. Woolf is merely, as she knew full well herself, making explicit theoretically a conclusion that she had noted in practice for some years, in Joyce and others. Huxley himself had employed this new and modern manner from the very outset of his career in stories like *The Farcical History of Richard Greenow* (1918) and novels like *Crome Yellow* (1921).

The first three chapters of *Brave New World*, especially, are masterfully composed in the indirect manner. Very little is heard; almost everything is overheard. To this manner Huxley also adds a refinement of his own devising, a technique perhaps best called counterpoint, since Huxley had used it most fully before in *Point Counter Point* (1929), though there are intimations of it as early as *Those Barren Leaves* (1925). This technique involves a simultaneous juxtaposition of different elements of the narrative, much as musical counterpoint means sounding different notes simultaneously with a cantus firmus. The result in music is, or should be, a complex harmony; in Huxley's fiction the result is, usually, a complex dissonance, a subtle and often brilliant cacophony of ironies. The third chapter of *Brave New World* is set up entirely in this kind of counterpoint, gathering together the various narrative strains of the first two chapters and juxtaposing them without any editorial comment, slowly at first and then with gathering momentum, climaxing in a crescendo that fuses snatches of Mond's lecture, Lenina's conversation with Fanny, Henry Foster's with

Benito Hoover, Bernard Marx's resentful thoughts, and bits of hypnopaedic wisdom.

The result is astonishing and far more effective in drawing us into the noisy and frantically joyless atmosphere of the new world state than pages of descriptive writing would have been. It is one of the most remarkable pieces of writing in the modern British novel.

Brave New World is modern, too, in another literary respect. It is shot through with literary allusions. Most of these allusions—such as the title and much of the conversation of the Savage—are to Shakespeare, but there are also more or less direct or indirect allusions to Shaw, Wells, T. S. Eliot, D. H. Lawrence, Voltaire, Rousseau, Thomas Gray, and Dante. The point of these allusions is not, I think, to show how clever and sophisticated and knowledgeable a writer Aldous Huxley is; the point is, rather, as in the poetry of T. S. Eliot—or Huxley's own poetry, for that matter—to reveal ironically the inadequacies of the present (or the present as contained in the future) by comparing it with the past. This is primarily how the literary allusions function in "The Waste Land" or in "Whispers of Immortality"—from which Huxley derives Lenina's peculiarly pneumatic sexuality—and that is also how they function primarily in *Brave New World*. The juxtaposition of Cleopatra with a bored modern woman who has nothing to do or of Spenser's and Goldsmith's lovers with the dreary amorous adventures of a modern secretary serves the same purpose as the juxtaposition of the love of Othello and Desdemona with that of the hero and heroine of the feely *Three Weeks in a Helicopter*, or even the love of Romeo and Juliet with that of Lenina and the Savage. The effect in both cases is that of a literary double exposure, which provides a simultaneous view of two quite distinct and yet horribly similar realities. The tension between the two—that which pulls them violently apart and at the same time pushes them violently together— produces a powerful irony, which is just what Eliot and Huxley want to produce. By means of this irony it then becomes possible for Huxley, or the narrator of his novel, to guide the reader's response without seeming to do so, without requiring any overt interference on his part. By merely hinting, for example, at the analogy between the Fordian state and Prospero's island, Huxley manages to convey ironically a disapproval of that state without ever having to voice it himself. And he can safely leave it to the reader to make the rest of the ironic identification; Mond is Prospero; Lenina is Miranda; the Savage is Ferdinand; Bernard Marx is Caliban. Or, if one prefers, Mond is a kind of Prospero and Alonso combined; the Savage, as befits his name, is Caliban, and his mother, Linda, is Sycorax; Lenina is a perverse Miranda and Bernard a strange Ferdinand. Or, to give another twist to it, the Director of

Hatcheries and Conditioning is a kind of Alonso who abandoned Linda and John to the desert; they in turn are, respectively, Prospero and Miranda, with their sexes reversed; the Indians and especially Pope are a kind of collective Caliban; Lenina, the aggressive lover, is a female Ferdinand, and Bernard a sort of rescuing Ariel. The same kind of ironic game can be played with Romeo and Juliet and Othello. In this way the ironies multiply until they become mind-boggling.

This is not to say that there is no direct narrative guidance in Huxley's novel. The reader is explicitly told, for example, that mental excess has produced in Helmholtz Watson's character the same results as a physical defect has in Bernard Marx. Or Bernard's psyche is analyzed for us in terms of an inferiority complex that finds its chief victims in his friends rather than his enemies. These are all acts of narrative interference and by no means isolated ones, but even so they are kept in the background and are, generally speaking, confined to attempts to make the psychological functioning of the characters more comprehensible.

Brave New World is a novel that is very carefully planned and put together. As Donald Watt has recently shown in his study [in *Journal of English and Germanic Philology* 77 (July 1978)] of Huxley's revisions in the typescript of *Brave New World*, a number of the best stylistic effects and one of the best scenes—the soma distribution riot—were afterthoughts, inserted by Huxley after he had finished the rest of the novel. This is not unusual for Huxley, who always revised his work thoroughly and in the process often came up with some of his best ideas. Just when Huxley started work on the novel is, however, not clear, though it is certain that the novel was finished, except for a few final touches, by the end of August 1931. *Brave New World* is first mentioned, though not by name, in Huxley's correspondence on May 18, 1931, and about a week later he wrote to his brother, Julian, that 'all I've been writing during the last month won't do and I must re-write in quite another way.' This clearly means that Huxley must have started the novel no later than the end of April or the beginning of May 1931. There is, however, some evidence to suggest that he may have been planning and perhaps even writing *Brave New World* as early as the latter part of 1930. For in an essay published in January 1931, entitled *Boundaries of Utopia*, Huxley describes a future world that in general—and in some striking details—anticipates the new world state. Served by mechanical domestics, Huxley writes in this essay,

> exploiting the incessant labour of mechanical slaves, the three-hundred-a-year men of the future state will enjoy an almost indefinite leisure. A system of transport, rapid, frequent and cheap [taxicopters and passenger rockets], will enable him to

move about the globe more freely than the emigrant rentier of the present age.... The theatres in which the egalitarians will enjoy the talkies, tasties, smellies, and feelies, the Corner Houses where they will eat their synthetic poached eggs on toast-substitute and drink their substitutes of coffee, will be prodigiously much vaster and more splendid than anything we know today.

Huxley concludes the essay by asserting that continuous progress is possible only on condition that the size of the population be limited and genetically improved.

The focus on leisure, rapid transport, amusements, synthetic substitutes, and genetic improvements in humans all suggest close links with *Brave New World*, so close indeed that it is difficult to believe that the novel was not already germinating in Huxley's mind and perhaps even on his typewriter. If this is true, then Huxley spent the better part of a year—nine or ten months—writing and rewriting *Brave New World*. If it is not true, then Huxley must have planned and written the novel in the astonishingly short time of a little less than four months. In either case, it is a remarkable achievement in a remarkably short time, though it should be remembered that utopian and anti-utopian ideas had been floating through Huxley's mind and popping up occasionally in his fiction since as early as 1921. However short a time the actual writing may have taken, there were clearly years of general preparation and preliminary thought that went into the novel.

One of the chief problems Huxley had with *Brave New World*, according to Donald Watt, was with the characters. On the evidence of the revisions, Watt concludes that Huxley seems first to have thought of making Bernard Marx the rebellious hero of the novel but then changed his mind and deliberately played him down into a kind of anti-hero. After rejecting the possibility of a heroic Bernard, Huxley next seems to have turned to the Savage as an alternative. According to Watt, there are in the typescript several indications, later revised or omitted, of the Savage's putting up or at least planning to put up violent resistance to the new world state, perhaps even of leading a kind of revolution against it. But in the process of rewriting the novel, Huxley also abandoned this idea in favor of having no hero at all, or of having only the vague adumbration of a hero in Helmholtz Watson.

Watt's analysis of the revisions in *Brave New World* is very helpful and interesting; he shows convincingly, I think, that Huxley was unable to make up his mind until very late in the composition of the novel just what direction he wanted the story and the leading male characters to take. From this uncertainty, however, I do not think it necessary to leap to the further conclusion that Huxley had difficulty in creating these characters themselves. Huxley's supposedly inadequate ability to create living characters, the result of his not being a congenital novelist, is a question that often arises in discussions of his fiction, and in connection with longer and more traditionally novelistic novels like *Point Counter Point* or *Eyeless in Gaza* (1936) appropriately so. But *Brave New World* is anything but a traditional novel in this sense. It is not a novel of character but a relatively short satirical tale, a fable, much like Voltaire's *Candide*. One hardly demands fully developed and round characters of *Candide*, nor should one of *Brave New World*.

This is all the more the case because the very nature of the new world state precludes the existence of fully developed characters. Juliets and Anna Kareninas, or Hamlets and Prince Vronskys, are by definition impossibilities in the new world state. To ask for them is to ask for a different world, the very world whose absence Huxley's novel so savagely laments. Character, after all, is shaped by suffering, and the new world state has abolished suffering in favor of a continuous, soma-stupefied, infantile happiness. In such an environment it is difficult to have characters who grow and develop and are alive.

Despite all this, it is surprising and noteworthy how vivid and even varied Huxley's characters are. With all their uniformly standardized conditioning, Alphas and Betas turn out to be by no means alike: the ambitious go-getter Henry Foster is different from his easy-going friend Benito Hoover; the unconventional and more pneumatic Lenina Crowne from the moralistic and rather less pneumatic Fanny Crowne; the resentful and ugly Bernard Marx from the handsome and intelligent Helmholtz Watson. Huxley, in fact, seems to work consistently and consciously in terms of contrastive/complementary pairs to suggest various possibilities of response to similar situations. So, too, Helmholtz and the Savage are another pair, as are the Savage and Mond, Mond and the DHC, Bernard and Henry Foster. The most fully developed instance of this pairing or doubling technique is the trip that Bernard and Lenina make to the Indian reservation, a trip that duplicates the one made some years earlier by the DHC and a particularly pneumatic Beta-Minus named Linda. Like the DHC, Bernard also leaves Lenina, another pneumatic Beta, (briefly) behind while returning to civilization, and during this interval she, too, is lusted after by a savage, much as Pope and the other Indians lust after Linda. Even the novel as a whole reveals a similar sort of doubling structure, with the new world state on the one hand and the Indian reservation on the other.

Within limits, the characters, even some of the minor and superficial characters like Henry Foster, are capable of revealing other and deeper facets of their personality. Returning with Lenina from the Stoke Poges Obstacle Golf Course, Henry Foster's helicopter suddenly shoots upward on a column of hot air rising from the Slough Crematorium. Lenina is delighted at this brief switchback, but Henry's tone was almost, for a moment, melancholy. 'Do you know what that switchback was?' he said. 'It was some human being finally and definitely disappearing. Going up in a squirt of hot gas. It would be curious to know who it was—a man or a woman, an Alpha or an Epsilon....' Henry quickly jolts himself out of this atypical mood and reverts to his normally obnoxious cheerfulness, but for an instant at least there was a glimpse of a real human being.

Much more than Henry, Bernard Marx and Helmholtz Watson are capable of complexity of response. The latter especially and partly through his contact with the Savage grows increasingly aware of himself as a separate human entity and of his dissatisfaction with the kind of life he had led hitherto. As an Emotional Engineer and contriver of slogans, Helmholtz has been very successful, as he also has been in the capacities of lover and sportsman; but he despises this success and seeks for a satisfaction for which he has no name and which he can only dimly conceive. He comes closest to expressing it in the poem that eventually leads to his exile, the poem in which an ideal and absent woman becomes more real to him—in the manner of Mallarme's flower that is absent from all bouquets—than any woman he has ever actually met.

In the end Helmholtz agrees to being sent into frigid exile in the Falkland Islands. The reason he chooses such a place rather than possible alternatives like Samoa or the Marquesas is because there he will not only have solitude but also a harsh climate in which to suffer and to gain new and very different experiences. His aim, however, is not, as some critics have suggested, to seek mystic experience; he simply wants to learn how to write better poetry. 'I should like a thoroughly bad climate,' he tells Mustapha Mond. 'I believe one would write better if the climate were bad. If there were a lot of wind and storms for example....' This hardly represents a search for mysticism and God; in this novel only the Savage, and he in only a very qualified way, can be described as seeking after such ends. Helmholtz merely wants more and better words. In the context of Huxley's work, he harks back to a character like Denis Stone in *Crome Yellow*, not forward to the pacifist Anthony Beavis in *Eyeless in Gaza* or in the inner-directed Propter in *After Many a Summer* (1939).

The same is true of Bernard Marx. Despite the apparent fact that Huxley once had more exalted intentions for him, Bernard belongs very much to the familiar Huxleyan category of the anti-hero, best exemplified perhaps by Theodore Gumbril, Jr., the so-called Complete Man of "Antic Hay" (1923). Like Gumbril, Bernard is able to envision and even seek after a love that is not merely sexual, but, like Gumbril again, his search is half-hearted. He is willing to settle for less because it is so much easier than trying to strive for more. Bernard is weak and cowardly and vain, much more so than Gumbril, and this makes him an unsympathetic character in a way that Gumbril is not. Nevertheless Bernard is undoubtedly capable of seeing the better, even if in the end he follows the worse.

Bernard is certainly a more fully developed character than Helmholtz; he is, in fact, with the exception of the Savage, the character about whom we know most in the entire novel. Just why this should be so is a question worth asking, just as it is worth asking why Bernard is the first of the novel's three malcontents to be brought to our attention.

Bernard's importance resides, I think, in his incapacity. The stability of the new world state can be threatened, it is clear, from above and from below. In the case of Helmholtz the threat is from above, from a surfeit of capacity; in Bernard's case it is from below, from a lack of sufficient capacity. This is not simply to say that Bernard is more stupid than Helmholtz, which he probably is, but rather that because of his physical inferiority he has developed a compulsive need to assert his superiority. It is this incapacity which, paradoxically, seems to make Bernard the more dangerous threat, for it compels him to rise to a position of power in his society; he wants to be accepted by his society, but only on his own terms, terms that are not acceptable in the long run if stability is to be maintained. Helmholtz, on the other hand, is a loner who really wants to have nothing to do with the society at all, and in this sense he represents much less of a threat. The Savage, on the other hand, though most violent and uncompromising in his hatred of and desire to destroy the new world state, is really no threat at all, for he originates from outside the society and is a kind of lusus naturae. There is never likely to be another Savage, but it is very probable that there will be or that there are more Bernards and Helmholtzes.

Both Bernard and Helmholtz are fairly complex characters. What is surprising, however, is that the same is true of Lenina Crowne. She seems at first to be nothing more than a pretty and addle-brained young woman without any emotional depth whatever. And at first it is true that this is all she is; but she changes in the course of the novel into something quite different. She changes because she falls in love.

The great irony of Lenina's falling in love is that she does not realize what it is that has happened to her; like Helmholtz she has no name for the new feeling and hence no way of conceiving or understanding what it is. She can only think of love in the physiological ways in which she has been conditioned to think of it; but her feeling is different.

So subtle is Huxley's portrayal of the change in Lenina that, as far as I know, no critic has ever commented on it. Yet Lenina is clearly predisposed from the very beginning to a love relationship that is not sanctioned by her society. As we learn from her conversation with Fanny, Lenina has been going with Henry Foster for four months without having had another man, and this in defiance of what she knows to be the properly promiscuous code of sexual behavior. When Fanny takes her up on this point of unconventionality, Lenina reacts almost truculently and replies that she jolly well [does not] see why there should have been anyone other than Henry. Her inability to see this error in her sexual ways is what predisposes her for the much greater and more intense feeling that she develops for the Savage.

The stages of her growing love for the Savage and her increasing mystification at what is happening within herself are handled with a brilliantly comic touch. There is the scene following Lenina's and the Savage's return from the feelies when the Savage sends her off in the taxicopter just as she is getting ready to seduce him. There is the touching moment when Lenina, who had once been terrified of pausing with Bernard to look at the sea and the moon over the Channel, now lingers for a moment to look at the moon, before being summoned by an irritated and uncomprehending Arch-Songster. There is Lenina's increasing impatience with the obtuseness of Henry Foster and his blundering solicitousness. There are the fond murmurings to herself of the Savage's name. There is the conference with Fanny as to what she should do about the Savage's strange coldness toward her. There is her blunt rejection of Fanny's advice to seek consolation with one of the millions of other men. There is the wonderful scene in which she seeks out the Savage alone in his apartment, discovers to her amazement that he loves her, sheds her clothing, and receives, to her even greater amazement, insults, blows, and a threat to kill. There is the final terrible scene at the lighthouse when Lenina steps out of the helicopter, looks at the Savage with an uncertain, imploring, almost abject smile, and then pressed both hands to her left side [i.e., to her heart], and on that peach-bright, doll-beautiful face of hers appeared a strangely incongruous expression of yearning distress. Her blue eyes seemed to grow larger, brighter; and suddenly two tears rolled down her cheeks. Again the Savage attacks her, this time with his whip, maddened by desire, by remorse, and by the horde of obscenely curious sightseers. In the end, however, desire triumphs and the Savage and Lenina consummate their love in an orgyporgian climax. When the Savage awakens to the memory of what has happened, he knows he cannot live with such defilement. For him the end is swift and tragic. For Lenina, however, there is no end; her tragedy—and for all the comedy and irony in which her love for the Savage is immersed, the word tragedy is not entirely inappropriate—her tragedy is that she has felt an emotion that she can never express or communicate or realize again.

The characters of *Brave New World*, it is safe to conclude, are not merely made of cardboard and papier-mache. That they are nonetheless not full and complete human beings is quite true; but for all the technology and conditioning and impulses toward uniformity, there is still something profoundly human about them. As Lenina's development in the novel indicates, it is possible, as it were, to scratch the plasticized doll-like surface of a citizen—at least of an Alpha or Beta citizen—of the new world state and draw actual blood. In this sense and to this degree, Huxley's vision of the perfectly planned future is not without hope; for all the genetic engineering and conditioning, basic humanity remains much the same as it always was. Its imperfections and its needs, even under such greatly altered conditions, inevitably reappear. And it is for this reason, I think, that Huxley's vision is so extraordinarily powerful and compelling; because in the people he portrays we can still somehow recognize ourselves. (pp. 13-24)

ROBERT S. BAKER

History and Psychology in the World State: Chapter 3

T he opening chapters of *Brave New World* introduce the reader to a future inspired not only by "Our Ford" but by "Our Freud" as well. Huxley had always insisted that any assessment of the ideals animating western European history after the First World War had to be based on "two tests, the historian's and the psychologist's." In his social novels of the twenties Huxley made extensive use of Freudian ideas, populating his narratives with characters twisted and warped by neurosis and, occasionally, by psychotic fears and anxieties. Characters like Spandrell in *Point Counter Point* or Joseph Stoyte in *After Many a Summer Dies the Swan* were, in Huxley's view, socially representative types that exemplified the traits of a culture in decline. In his novels he drew upon Freudian psychoanalysis and "the Freudian 'complexes' for which family relationships are responsible." In *Brave New World* he utilizes Freudian concepts in his characterization of John, the Savage, but in the introductory chapters the educational techniques of the World State are grounded in the behaviorist psychology of Ivan Pavlov and J. B. Watson discussed earlier.

Watson's application of the principles of mechanistic science to psychology led to a reduction of human behavior to the laws of physics and chemistry. Such predictable and testable laws underlay Watson's psychology, which was premised on the belief that mind or consciousness was confined to

From Brave New World: *History, Science, and Dystopia.* © 1990 by G.K. Hall & Co.

physiological responses to external stimuli. Bertrand Russell, in *The Scientific Outlook*, regarded such an emphasis on the external stimulation of an essentially passive mind (i.e., conditioning) as a technique for acquiring power. Accordingly, the "menacing geniality" of the Director of Hatcheries suggests the peculiar combination of benign yet sinister coercion that informs all of the activities of the World State.

The introductory chapters describe a world in which the potentially refractory individual is socialized through behaviorist techniques of psychological conditioning. In chapter 2 the students are taken to the "Neo-Pavlovian Conditioning Rooms" where children are subjected to electric shocks and shrieking sirens in an effort to induce an "instinctive hatred of books and flowers" and in which the "reflexes" are "unalterably conditioned" (23). The final result of such "instruments of social stability" as behaviorist techniques is epitomized in the sleep teaching or "hypnopaedic" inculcation of "Elementary Class Consciousness" (30). Again, politics and science are merged as Huxley satirically conflates what in "The New Romanticism" he described as the Soviet communist's devotion to mechanistic science with what the Marxist finds most repulsive in capitalism, the class system. At the same time, Huxley invokes the capitalist's belief in Fordian mass production criticized in "The Outlook for American Culture" with the highly centralized bureaucracy characteristic of Soviet society. The result is dystopian society combining what Huxley regarded as the most dangerous tendencies within the Soviet Union and the United States of the late twenties and early thirties—a combination of excessive reliance on technology and collectivist values resulting in a mechanized, rationalized society. Within such a state, Bernard's surname can be Marx and the woman he desires can be called Lenina, while both venerate the memory of "Our Ford."

The Central London Hatchery is not simply a symbol of a technology perverted to bad ends—the creation of a scientifically determined race of compliant automatons. Such a stifling of human possibilities as a result of Pavlovian and Watsonian techniques is intrinsically political in that systematized behaviorist conditioning is a form of coercion set in motion by specialists in order to ensure social and political stability. The Director appeals to "high economic policy" as the ultimate justification of the World State's manipulative practices. The need to control the consumption of "manufactured articles" through the "socializing force" of genetic engineering, Taylorization, and behaviorist conditioning is one of the principal reasons for the existence of the Director's laboratories. His one moment of genuine excitement during his lecture occurs when, at the end, he suddenly exults, "But all these suggestions are *our* suggestions! ...

Suggestions from the State" (32). This assertion of the primacy of the state is an assertion about power and its sources, and leads to the appearance of "his fordship Mustapha Mond" at the beginning of the crucial third chapter.

The World State is governed by a committee. Mond is one of the ten World Controllers, and his appearance signals a shift in Huxley's use of psychology in *Brave New World*. Mond, like the Director, is a technical specialist, a scientist who fully endorses the behaviorist conditioning on which the security of the World State rests. In Mond's version of history, Freudian neurosis and destructively irrational or abnormal behavior are to be found only in what he calls the "terrible" past, before the introduction of universal conditioning techniques. In brief, Watsonian behaviorism is the stable, pacified present; Freudian psychosis was characteristic of human history before the establishment of Mond's utopia. The Savage, introduced later, who lives outside of the World State, is neurotic and irrationally violent for this, reason; he lives in a precarious state of unconditioned freedom.

Mustapha Mond uses Freudian categories of thought solely in order to condemn the past. His very first words in *Brave New World* compose a sweeping repudiation of the past, in particular, its inability to come to terms with human sexuality and erotic desire. Just before Mond's appearance, the Director and his students, having completed their tour of the Hatchery, walk outside to observe the games of the children—including "erotic play." The Director uses the occasion to muse on history, warning his students that "when you're not accustomed to history, most facts about the past *do* sound incredible" (36). The incredible fact that he proceeds to reveal is that erotic play between children was once regarded as abnormal. As his students gape in disbelief and ask what the results were, Mustapha Mond appears for the first time and announces, "The results were terrible" (37).

Mond's verdict on nonutopian history introduces the historical summary characteristic of the modern dystopia. In the main section of chapter 3, subdivided into 123 smaller units, Huxley contrasts the stable behaviorist present of the World State with its unstable neurotic past by means of an assortment of voices. Throughout this section the voice of the anonymous third person narrator is supplemented by the voices of major characters like Bernard Marx and Lenina Crowne, and minor figures like Henry Foster and Fanny. The result is a medley of social perspectives that collectively express the social texture of World State society. As the chapter proceeds, however, the reader becomes aware of the increasingly dominant voice of the World Controller, Mustapha Mond. When collated, Mond's observations can be seen to compose a fragmented but sufficiently continuous record of history prior to the establishment of his scientific utopia. Equally important—and illustrative of Huxley's belief in the close interrelationship between psychology and history—Mond's remarks are inspired by a discussion of sexuality, erotic desire, and the nuclear family as a social institution.

Like Gibbon in his *Decline and Fall of the Roman Empire*, Mond views history as "little more than the register of the crimes, follies, and misfortunes of mankind." He simply discards world history from the ancient Middle East ("Harappa ... Ur of the Chaldees ... Thebes and Babylon and Cnossos and Mycenae") up to "the pre-moderns," just prior to the founding of the World State. He rejects everything, including literature, music, art, and philosophy. For Mond, the World State is a state without a past, continuous with nothing beyond itself. Preutopian history he interprets as a turbulent record of violence, pathology, and irrational excess. "That's why you're taught no history," he informs the students. But, like the Director, he immediately contradicts himself, adding, "but now the time has come" for a history lesson.

The Director is surprised at Mond's willingness to raise the forbidden subject, and remembers the "strange rumours of old forbidden books hidden in a safe in the Controller's study" (39). Like many of the inhabitants of the World State, Mond cannot completely control his fascination with time and history. He begins his lecture of fallen or pre-utopian mankind with, in his view, the quintessential Eve, "a viviparous mother" (40), that is, a symbol of natural child-bearing. The family and its basis in maternity have been rendered obsolete by World State technology. They have been banished as a source of economic as well as psychological instability. Mond defines the family as the creation of the mother, a site of aberrancy and disease "as squalid psychically as physically." The home of pre-modern times he describes as "an understerilized prison" (42), an airless rabbit hole, "hot with the frictions of tightly packed life, reeking with emotion. What suffocating intimacies, what dangerous, insane, obscene relationships between the members of the family group" (42). At the center stands the mother, "maniacally" infecting her children with "every kind of perversion from sadism to chastity" (44). Mond's disgust with familial relationships can be traced to the Freudian assessment of the family and what Huxley called, as noted earlier, those "Freudian 'complexes' for which family relationships are responsible." The reference to sadism and chastity is important because the Savage, as we shall see, suffers from a sadistic obsession with sexual chastity as a result of his mother's influence.

Mond loathes the image of the mother, and while he inveighs against it as a source of incapacitating neurosis, the voice of Lenina Crowne appears in the text for the first time. Lenina is the new woman, sexually promiscuous, free of family responsibilities, and conditioned to feel only aversion for monogamous relationships. Her first remarks are part of a discussion with her friend Fanny on the advisability of a Pregnancy Substitute; but the conversation shifts to Lenina's perplexing tendency to see the same man for extended periods of time. In a society where undiscriminating promiscuity is a virtue, Lenina's preference for long-drawn-out affairs with only one male is regarded as perversely immoral. While Fanny warns Lenina about her antisocial behavior, Mustapha Mond continues his attack on "mother, monogamy, [and] romance" (47), arguing that such a stress on loyalty and romantic love fostered neurosis and "endless isolating pain." What Mond fears in monogamous love is its intensity of feeling, because such emotional energy encouraged the "instability" of individualism. This is the all-important thematic point in Mond's diatribes against romantic love and the family; he fears the sense of individual identity fed and nurtured by subjective feelings.

Mond's repudiation of strong or concentrated feeling is linked to the essential ideological principle on which the World State is founded. For the World Controller, history is a record of abnormal pathology, an immense case history of neurotic and psychotic behavior. Society is a patient who must be tranquilized, calmed, rendered passive and stable, hence the mass distributions of the drug *soma*. Mond identifies stability as "the primal and ultimate need" (44), defining it as a state of "calm well-being." The reason he regards the family as a threat to such placid contentedness lies in his distinctly Freudian preoccupation with the violent consequences of frustrated desire and repression. The family is indicted as the scene of destabilizing impulses born of repressed desires, irrationally intense emotion, and egocentric rivalry. The resulting Freudian complexes are to be laid to rest by means of behaviorist conditioning. These two irreconcilable psychologies are brought together in *Brave New World* in such a way that one provides the diagnosis, the other, the cure.

In Huxley's view Freudian depth psychology turned on the pivotal concept of covert or unconscious mental activity, especially the idea of unconscious desire that could be repressed and thus become productive of inner turmoil and irrational behavior. Within Mustapha Mond's world of conditioned serenity and social stability, the single enemy is arrested desire, symbolized by the decanted infant howling for his bottle. What Mond and his bureaucratic technicians fear is the irrational intensity of raw desiring emotion. "Feeling lurks in that interval of time between desire and its consummation" (51), Mond says, and he is dedicated to obliterating the moment of unsatisfied desire. The World State is, after all, utopia. By removing the moment of unconsummated desire, Mond will eliminate intense emotion itself, because strong emotion is born of frustrated desire. By disposing of vital emotion he will have extinguished selfhood or personal identity, thus ensuring both personal and social stability.

In the interwar period the key texts for such an anxious perspective on human behavior in relation to history and society were Freud's *Civilization and its Discontents* and *The Future of an Illusion*. Freud's philosophy of history was a relatively somber one, stressing the irrational intensity of human desires and appetites and the resulting need for coercion, for the renunciation of instinctual desire and its sublimation in creative work. Religion he dismissed as a mass delusion, arguing that it had to be supplanted by science. The limited degree of progress open to humanity was dependent on humanity's capacity for collective self-discipline, especially the renunciation of the more powerful and hence more destructive forms of erotic desire. Such a process of disciplined control could be achieved by means of sublimation, that is, the modification, deflection, and taming of appetitive energies by channeling them into socially acceptable and stabilizing forms of activity (i.e., art, science, technology, etc.). Accordingly, the goal of history was the establishment of scientific consciousness in the manner of H. G. Wells's *Men Like Gods*. The intellectual ascendancy of the scientific state of mind would control and harness humanity's more irrational psychological drives, and that, in turn, could lead to control of both the social and natural environment. But Freud also believed that utopia was a dream; the barbaric past and the destructive psychic impulses that energized it are always present, always a potential threat to social and individual harmony. Mustapha Mond's World State is premised on this darker view of human potentiality in which Wells's scientific rationalist like the Utopian Urthred is always in danger of succumbing to the "ancestral man-ape" within.

In his lecture to the Director's students Mond employs the simple metaphor of water under pressure to illustrate his understanding of the dynamics of human desire, observing that the more holes are punched in a water pipe, the weaker the pressure of each individual leak. Mond's answer to destructively intense desire is to let off the pressure wherever possible, in systematically controlled ways. His view of civilization is essentially permissive, especially in the sphere of sexuality. Sexual promiscuity is held up as a normal human activity; indeed, he regards it as a socially beneficial mode of behavior in a society where sensual appetite is pandered to in a scientifically coordinated way. Mond promises the reduction of the "interval of time between desire and its consummation" through the universal availability of the objects of desire. To do this on a large scale, the objects are commodified; the women of his utopia are sexual objects—as are the men—in a society "where every one belongs to every one else." What appetites remain are neutralized by drugs and sophisticated forms of entertainment, like the Feelies. What is absent in the World State is any form of self-denial, especially the sublimation or deflection of appetitive energy into the creation of art, literature, music, or genuinely creative science. Such activities would require the deferral or renunciation of sensual desire, and Mond fears such repression as productive of neurosis and violent emotion. "Impulse arrested," he warns the students, "spills over, and the flood is feeling, the flood is passion, the flood is even madness: it depends on the force of the current, the height and strength of the barrier. The unchecked stream flows smoothly down its appointed channels into a calm well-being" (50). The government of the World State clearly prefers the "unchecked stream" of satisfied desire and its resulting social order of hedonistic conformity.

Mond's summary of "pre-modern history," then, is history viewed as a case record of pathological violence born of socially uncoordinated energies. In the "new era" such anarchic impulses are not rechanneled into art or scientific research but simply damped down by means of drugs or placated by an ethic of immediate satisfaction. The past is terrible because unstable. Human civilization, informed by neurotic aims and ambitions, may have produced the paintings of Michelangelo and the plays of Shakespeare, but at too high a price. As the Fordian apologist for the "interests of industry" and the Freudian advocate of the pleasure principle, Mond emphasizes only the disruptive and anarchic aspects of history. He has no faith in humanity's capacity for self-disciplined and creative labor, and this pessimism is reflected in his history of the "pre-modern" era. As in Wells's *The Sleeper Awakes* or Zamiatin's *We*, the period of history prior to the establishment of utopia is one of increasing civil violence and widespread social instability. Mond's chronology can be collated as follows:

A.F. 1 (1908)	The opening date of the new era. The introduction of Our Ford's first Model T (1908). Period of liberalism and the appearance of "the first reformers."
A.F. 141 (2049)	Outbreak of "The Nine Years' War" followed by "the great Economic Collapse." Period of Russian ecological warfare including the poisoning of rivers and the anthrax bombing of Germany and France.

A.F. 150	The beginning of "World Control."
(2058)	The "conscription of consumption" followed by a period of social restiveness and instability.
	The rise of "Conscientious objection and [a] back to nature movement."
	The reaction to liberal protest movements including the Golders Green massacre of "Simple Lifers" and the British Museum Massacre.
	Abandonment of force by the World Controllers.
	Period of an antihistory movement and social reeducation including intensive propaganda directed against viviparous reproduction and a "campaign against the Past."
	Closing of museums.
	Suppression of all books published before A.F. 150.
A.F. 178 (2086)	Government drive to discover a socially useful narcotic without damaging side effects.
	Establishment of special programs in pharmacology and biochemistry.
A.F. 184 (2092)	The discovery of *soma*.
A.F. 473 (2381)	The Cyprus Experiment: establishment of a wholly Alpha community.
A.F. 478 (2386)	Civil War in Cyprus. Nineteen thousand Alphas killed.
A.F. 482 (2390)	The Ireland Experiment (increased leisure time and four-hour work week).
A.F. 632 (2540)	The present of *Brave New World*.

Mond's chronicle of the foundation of the new era highlights two aspects of World State ideology. First, it stresses the attempt to obliterate all knowledge of the past, the antihistory movement reflecting the new era's need to seize control of the historical record, not to rewrite it, as in Orwell's *Nineteen Eighty-Four*, but to remove the concept of history itself from human consciousness. Second, in the references to the "back to nature movement" and the emphasis on technological experimentation, it foregrounds the typical dystopian opposition between nature and reason. Equally important, Mond's chronicle does not suggest a progressive unfolding of human potentiality (as in Wells's *Men Like Gods*). The final social experiments in Cyprus and Ireland are indicative of human limits, of boundaries beyond which humanity cannot develop. The World State is not the beginning of a new period of evolving and progressing civilization that Wells had celebrated in *Men Like Gods*. Rather, it is a massive socioeconomic improvisation marking the final termination of history. It is premised on the futility of history and offers in its stead what amounts to the apocalyptic ushering in of a society so authoritarian and immobile that historical progress has been halted, rather like a river frozen in its bed. This achievement of, in Mond's words, "the stablest equilibrium in history" (272) is attributable to a paralysis of historical process that extends to the temporal experience of the individual citizen, where birth most often leads to arrested development, and where life involves a mindless dedication to the immediate present. Neither past nor future has meaning.

Mond's chronicle, with its emphasis on the linear, sequential nature of time and the irrationality of past history, brings into sharper focus the principal anxiety of the World State: the disruptive nature of time itself. It is not just the cultural past and the study of history that is banished from Mond's dystopia. Temporal process is regarded as a condition to be carefully calibrated and controlled. The hypnopaedic sentence, "Ending is better than mending," that is whispered into the ears of sleeping children at the Hatchery is typical in this respect. The statement is an economic principle that encourages commodity consumption rather than a more frugal concern with wasteful and unnecessary expenditure. But "ending" is also a temporal concept suggesting the principal aim of World State ideology: the ending of desire in immediate satisfaction, the ending of history in the new era where future progress ("mending") is irrelevant.

Mond's "now" of the World State involves a complete immersion in present time. If desire is deferred then dissatisfaction persists in time with— as Mond believes—all of its attendant frustrations and unstable emotions. "Now," he proclaims "the old men work, the old men copulate, the old men *have no time*, no leisure from pleasure, *not a moment* to sit down and think" (66–67; emphasis added). The final escape from time is the drug *soma*, defined by Mond as "a dark eternity," that is, as inducing an inherently timeless state of mind. What Mond fears is the appearance of "a crevice of time," unexpectedly yawning "in the solid substance" of World State materialism (67). He asks his audience, "Has any of you been compelled to live through a long time-interval between the consciousness of a desire and its fulfillment?" (52). Such an interval or "crevice of time" is a space in which the mind can expand and develop, in which desire can be rechanneled or sublimated. It is also a site of disruptive emotion or longing. Bernard Marx is viewed with suspicion by Fanny because "he spends most of his time by himself" (52).

The endeavor of the technocrats "to conquer old age" (65) is part of a wider, more subtle agenda that would force humanity to alter profoundly its experience of time. The World State, then, is, in a manner of speaking, a new time zone where characters remain constant throughout a whole lifetime, where the stages of birth, maturity, and aging no longer have meaning, and where historical process has simply ended. It is, accordingly, appropriate that the collage of voices composing chapter 3, including Mond's dominant voice, should end with the novel's presiding symbol of the World State's technological dominance of time: "Slowly, majestically, with a faint humming of machinery, the Conveyors moved forward, thirty-three centimeters an hour" (67). This final image of the conquest of natural childbirth is also a symbol of the victory over natural time—or at least what can be called the unmanipulated temporal experience characteristic of the pre-modern age so thoroughly condemned by Mond. Bernard Marx is introduced to the reader as an error in World State calibrations, someone for whom the "interval of time between desire and its consummation" is continually widening. Out of step with his fellow citizens, he threatens to disrupt the stately movement of the Fordian production line with distinctly Freudian disturbances.

GEORGE WOODCOCK

Brave New World: *Overview*

Aldous Huxley was fascinated throughout his career by the idea of Utopia, the society in which change has settled down into a stasis of perfection. In his last novel, *Island*, he saw it as a benign perfection in a peaceful and ecologically aware society guided by mystics. But in his much better known *Brave New World*, published three decades before in 1932, he saw it as a malign society controlled by technocrats whose aim is complete happiness, but in whose hands happiness is equated with the total absence of freedom.

Brave New World is both a fantasy about the future and a satire on present trends. And in both roles it carries conviction because of the expert and convincing handling of detail to create a plausible world. It is England 600 years ahead, and Huxley has been wise enough not to change it beyond recognition. It is the country we know and a different world, and this paradox sustains our attention.

The society of the future is a parody of Plato's republic, with a small group of World Controllers ruling five castes of subjects, divided not merely socially but biologically, since they have been conditioned to their future tasks in the bottles where they were bred. To preserve happiness, the World Controllers discard everything that might provoke either thought or passion. The world's stable now [says Mustapha Mond, Controller for England]. People are happy; they get what they want, and they never want what they

From *Reference Guide to English Literature, 2nd Edition.* © 1991 by St. James Press.

can't get. They're well off; they're safe; they're never ill; they're not afraid of death; they're blissfully ignorant of passion and old age; they're plagued with no mothers or fathers; they've got no wives, or children, or lovers to feel strongly about; they're so conditioned that they practically can't help behaving as they ought to behave.

There is no need for violent or overt repression. Men are so conditioned from the time the spermatazoon enters the egg in the Hatchery that there is little chance of their breaking into rebellion; if they do become discontented there are always drugs to waft them into the heavens of restorative illusion. Thus the Controllers are able to govern with a softly firm hand; the police use whiffs of anaesthetic instead of truncheons, and those over-brilliant individuals who do not fit the established pattern are allowed to indulge their heretical notions in the intellectual quarantine of exile.

The daily lives of the conditioned inhabitants of the brave new world are passed in a carefully regulated pattern of production and consumption. Since it was found that too much leisure created restlessness, scientists are discouraged from devising labour-saving inventions, and the working day is followed by gregarious pleasures so organised that elaborate machinery is needed and maximum consumption is encouraged. Complete freedom of sexual behaviour, plus the availability of drugs, provide release from all ordinary frustrations. The abolition of viviparous birth has made families and all other permanent attachments unnecessary; individuals have become merely cells, each occupying his special position in the carefully differentiated fabric of society.

All this would not make a novel of its own. Huxley brings it to life by showing the hidden perils of any attempt at a perfect society. The higher castes, the Alphas and Betas, cannot be as closely conditioned as the worker castes, because their tasks involve intelligence and the occasional need to use judgment, and even the best conditioning is not foolproof. So we get individualists like the stunted Bernard Marx who has a heretical longing for solitude, like Lenina Crowne who is inclined to remain too constant in her attachments, like Helmholtz Watson who secretly writes forbidden poems about the self instead of slogans for the state.

The crisis in the life of these three misfits is provoked by a journey into unfamiliarity. Bernard takes Lenina on a trip to the reservation for primitive people. There they discover a woman from their own society who was lost years ago and since then has lived and brought up a normally born child among the Indians. The young man—John—is not only a savage; he has also acquired a copy of Shakespeare, which, with the mixed heathen-Christian native cults, has enriched his language and shaped his outlook. In our sense he is far more "cultured," if not more "civilized," than the Utopians.

Bernard brings the savage back to London, where he creates a sensation by his baroque behavior and Elizabethan speech. On Bernard and Helmholtz he has the effect of crystallizing their sense of difference from society, while Lenina lapses into an old-fashioned attachment to the savage, who meanwhile has conceived a romantic attachment to her.

Bernard, Helmholtz, and the savage create a minor rebellion by interrupting a distribution of soma (a drug) to the workers. Bernard and Helmholtz are exiled to join those who have shown themselves unreliable (the real intellectual élite of the brave new world). The savage is forbidden to join them, because the Controllers wish to continue the experiment of subjecting him to "civilization." Since he cannot go home, the savage tries to hide out in the Surrey countryside, but Utopia's equivalent of newshounds discover him, and the fervent pleasure-seekers of the brave new world, hearing that he is flogging himself like a Mexican penitent, descend on him in their helicopters. Lenina is foremost among them. There is a great orgy in which he first whips and then possesses her. The next day, revolted by Utopia and his surrender to its seductions, he hangs himself. It is the savage who alone, since he is the only character conscious of the nature of tragedy, can embody the tragic possibilities of man's future.

JUNE DEERY

Technology and Gender
in Aldous Huxley's Alternative (?) Worlds

Technology is old, older than science, yet there has been greater technological advance this century than in all of previously recorded history. According to Aldous Huxley, this phenomenon is remarkable also for its lack of impact on twentieth-century literature. Some of his own works are exceptions, particularly the utopian *Brave New World* (1932)—now a byword for nightmarish technocracy—and the other alternative worlds of *Ape and Essence* (1949) and *Island* (1962). But just how alternative are these worlds? In order to determine this, I shall examine Huxley's portrayal, not only of the impact of technology on the social body as a whole, but also its impact on the female citizen in particular in each of these texts.

To utopianize is to clear a space, to examine fundamentals, and, in making a selection of what is most vital in an autonomously constructed society, what the author omits is often as interesting as what is included; so it is with Huxley on female status. Technology, on the other hand, has been an important part of the utopian tradition since Francis Bacon. Yet Huxley was not one who thought technology alone would usher in the New Jerusalem, and one of the reasons he wrote *Brave New World* was to respond to the high-tech, steel paradises associated with H. G. Wells.[1]

In *Brave New World*, which began as a parody of Wells's *Men Like Gods* (Plimpton 198), Huxley has a good deal of fun with technological

From *Extrapolation* 33, 3. © 1992 by *Extrapolation*.

innovations and anticipates several trends. Here technology underpins the whole of society and is worshiped in the name of Ford.[2] In detailing its various manifestations, Huxley approaches the technological fetishism of science fiction, yet there is not enough hard science for his accuracy to be tested. Fortunately, he has a happy knack for coining convincing terminology and at once giving it an air of familiarity.

In this novel, the notion of mass production is applied with a vengeance, being extended to consumers as well as consumer items. The entire society is organized along Fordian (or Taylorian) lines: so vital is Ford, in fact, that the calender dates from his first model-T car. Practically everything is not only disposable but synthetic: the highest praise accorded to any product is that it is "real...-surrogate" (52). Citizens are happiest in a neon-lit, artificial environment where nature is as far as possible ignored (76), their entertainment being provided by that new art form born of technology: the cinema. The helicopters the upper-class characters commonly use for private transport were, it is worth remembering, only at an experiment stage when this text was being written, and the effect of rapid transport on people's lives, the fast pace and the regimentation, was also just beginning to be felt. Huxley's characters remark if a transatlantic rocket-plane is but a few minutes late.

> "There's the Red Rocket," said Henry, "just come in from New York." Looking at his watch. "Seven minutes behind time," he added, and shook his head. "These Atlantic services—they're really scandalously unpunctual." (61)

Leaving aside this early portrayal of rocket technology, perhaps we forget that even the technology for standardizing World Time had been developed only twenty years earlier in 1912.[3] In other areas, Huxley anticipates everything from cloning, which only began with animals in the 1950's, to so-called test-tube babies, first successful in 1978, years after Huxley's death. The fact that Huxley's brother Julian and family friends such as the Haldanes were top biologists made Huxley privy to many current and anticipated developments.[4] In turn, *Brave New World* spurred on research in certain fields, according to the testimony of some biologists (McLaughlin 62), But the really big revolution, Huxley predicts, is not only in bio-but also psycho-technology, and here again he was ahead of his time.

The scientific attitude in the new world is rigidly Baconian. Fordian researchers view themselves as conquistadors who, in an ecstasy of quantification, are out to put nature in its place. They delight because they have graduated from "the realm of mere slavish imitation of nature into the much more interesting world of human invention" (12). All of this is of course regarded as appallingly hubristic by the author. Note how the process of growing the human fetus is described as dependent on "massive doses of hog's stomach extract and foetal foal's liver" (11). And the idea of deliberately disabling a future human being, which is common practice on this production line, is surely repugnant, as is the sadistic postnatal conditioning with electric shocks (20), all in the Procrustian determination to fit the individual human being to the State's requirements.

But to what ends exactly? This is the question Huxley would have us append to every discussion of technological means. In this case the aim is simply to keep the machinery turning and maintain all citizens, male and female, in a state of calm though superficial contentment. Each has a limited and specialized function in the great mechanism of the State, the whole being lubricated by synthetic drugs. Any one individual knows very little about anything beyond his or her own specialized task. For example, Linda used to inject chemicals into test tubes, but when her son asks where chemicals come from she can only reply: "Well, I don't know. You get them out of bottles. And when the bottles are empty, you send up to the Chemical Store for more" (132). Interestingly, in *Brave New World* even science has been replaced by technology. "Pure" research has been muzzled to create a permanent state of normal science (Kuhn 181) where technologists deal only with immediate problems and none risk theoretical or metaphysical upsets (BNW 23-32). In accordance with Fordism, truth and beauty have been replaced by comfort and one brand of "happiness for all, a happiness which to Huxley signals humanity's quiet and irreversible self-destruction.

But how does technology impact on female experience in particular? In answering this, one uncovers a gender bias in Huxley's technocracy, though such a bias is nowhere explicitly stated as a founding principle. We quickly learn that classes are rigidly defined, but there is nothing to suggest that within each class women are to be regarded as inferior to men. In practice, however, after the 200 meter mark when sex is discovered (11), citizens appear to be treated differently according to gender, and the difference often means inequality, with women being assigned the lower status. In some instances, Huxley both recognizes the bias in the system and explicitly condemns it, but in other instances it is a function of his own perspective and he is oblivious to the inequalities his illustration introduces.

Interestingly, it is possible to argue that in some areas, despite its being a dystopia, *Brave New World* offers women a better deal than the contemporary British society of the 1930s. There is no housework, no wifely subjugation, no need to balance children and a career. And if women do not appear to have the vote (which in Britain they had gained only six years earlier), then neither do the men, for all are equally disfranchised in this society.[5] Yet, for all this, if we compare their position to that of men in *Brave New World*, women are less well off. A dystopia is, of course, a negative picture, but this does not imply a simple reversal, when what appears to be approved is rally condemned and vice versa. If women appear to have achieved a modicum of freedom, this is not frowned upon by the author, but then the disadvantages that they in particular face are not necessarily condemned either. The picture is much more complex. In fact, Huxley has often confused his readers because not everything in, *Brave New World* is viewed as unpalatable. The point here being that one of the things Huxley does not always portray as objectionable is woman's relatively inferior role.

On occasion, he does recognize and explicitly criticize women's treatment in this society. This is most evident in his portrayal of sexual interplay. At first, the general promiscuity is seen as amusingly novel, and there is no serious discussion of what it reveals about a woman's position relative to men. The anonymous narrator is not explicitly gendered. Indeed, Huxley's desire to create a sense of lifeless uniformity means the language he employs is often less gendered than one might expect in a text of this period. Yet our first view of a woman is undoubtedly through male eyes, and the first comment is on her sexual attractiveness (15), or, from T.S Eliot, her "pneumatic" appeal (44).[6] We subsequently learn that the correct etiquette is for a man to pat a woman on the behind and murmur "charming" while she returns a deferential smile (15). This sort of behavior rapidly becomes less amusing when it is pointed out that in this society women are seen, and regard themselves, as "meat", and (as in our society) meat which must be lean, not fat. While chewing their sex-hormone gum (we don't see women using these stimulants), men compare different women as sexual partners and seem to strengthen their own bonding by recommending previous lovers. "Yes, I really do advise you to try her,' Henry Foster was saying.... "But, my dear chap, you're welcome, I assure you" (46). According to Huxley's description, men tend to ask women out on dates, and it is they who drive the helicopters (this, I think, is crucial). All of this may be because upper-class men appear to date lower-class women, a class difference which en-genders another hierarchy. But as to why this is so or how common it is, we are given no clue. What we do witness is that this pattern makes it difficult for the female to refuse her body to her higher caste sexual partner. (For women, it seems, "free love" means always having to say yes). Thus Lenina, in love with someone else, has to dope herself before having sex with a highly-placed male (181), but we don't see a man prostituting himself in this fashion. Bernard, the misfit, finds this attitude towards women repugnant and expresses his distaste at the men's locker room conversation: "'Talking about her as though she were a bit of meat.' Bernard ground his teeth. 'Have her here, have her there. Like mutton. Degrading her to so much mutton.'" (45). It is an attitude that is reinforced in the world of entertainment, if the film Huxley chooses to describe is anything to go by. This latest movie, or "feely," depicts a Beta blonde who, after being abducted by a lower-class black male, is rescued by a trio of upper-class white males and, in gratitude, becomes the mistress of all three of them (171), thus preserving both a gender and, it seems, racial hierarchy. Off the screen too, we note that the popularly admired type is the athletic, powerful, sociable "he-man" who always gets his girl (66-67). And it is always "he" and who gets his "girl" in this hermetically heterosexual society.[7]

It may be that Huxley is deliberately using the movie to highlight these biases, and it may be that he generally depicts a high-class male soliciting a lower-class female in order to disclose a gender inequality. Certainly there is some distaste for the view of women as sexual "meat," but it may also be, and I think this is more likely, that men propositioning women and men driving helicopters is merely an unthinking mirroring of Huxley's own society. There are occasions when one cannot be sure the Huxley recognizes or would have us recognize instances of sexual discrimination which appear embedded in the system; for example, as opposed to the "Girls' Dressing-Room" (35), the men emerge from the upper-class "Alpha Changing Rooms" (57). This might be interpreted as a revelation that this society regards men not only as superior but also as the norm. However, none of this reading is actually underscored in the text, and so we are at a loss to decide whether the bias is the dystopians' or Huxley's.

There are other instances of simple neglect. Thus, we can assume that numerous upper-class females exist somewhere in this society—there is nothing which precludes this—but in Huxley's account we get only a brief glance of one of them—the headmistress at Eton. Even here we encounter her when she is in a position of need relative to the Alpha-Plus male who approaches her (164), and we note that her superior is a male Provost (163). The name of this upper-class female is, incidentally, "Miss" Keate, surely an anachronistic form of address in a society where there is no marriage. Perhaps Huxley has forgotten this in his desire to recreate the stereotype of the spinsterish headmistress, the woman who achieves position only by forfeiting her "true femininity."

In other cases it is even clearer that the gender bias is not, in fact, part of the dystopian system but is a function of Huxley's subsequent and unmindful portrayal of certain details once the society's basic principles have been established. Obviously there can be no denunciation where there isn't even a recognition of injustice. Rather, what we find is an automatic importation of the sexist norms of Huxley's own society into the imagined world. It is not a question of deliberately portraying the dystopia, "the bad place," as objectionable because, among other things, it treats women unfairly relative to men. Instead, the unequal treatment is frequently attributable to Huxley's own viewpoint. Rarely is the citizen in any dystopia in an enviable situation, but Huxley's portrayal goes further by placing women in an even lower position than men, and by not making a point of it. In short, there are many unattractive features of this society, but women's lack of position is not foregrounded as one of them.

Though there is nothing we know of in the dystopian constitution to bar them, Huxley simply fails to offer examples of women in power. The World Controller, the Director of Hatcheries and Conditioning, the Arch-Community Songster—all are men. There is even an male Assistant Director of Predestination (1), with the male gods of Ford and Freud hovering above. All of the women we encounter are slight characters, more objects than subjects, who are not able to break through the constraints of their society, much less Huxley's two-dimensional characterization, as some of the men begin to do. Although Kumar suggests that Lenina's falling in love might be the only door to overturning the present regime (287), it is such a static, one might almost say apolitical, society that it is difficult to see any possibility of upsetting the status quo to benefit either men or women.

Again, take the position, an important one in this society, of the technologist. The senior figures we encounter are invariably male. It is hardly surprising that, as recent studies have shown, there is a masculinity bias at the roots of modern science, both as an enterprise and worldview[8]; what *Brave New World* does is simply reflect and perpetuate this tradition. We note that the novel opens with knowledge being handed on from senior males to younger male students. The association of technology with masculinity is reinforced by the fact that the sign for males in this society happens to be identical to the divine symbol of Fordian technology, the T. However, this identification is never explicitly remarked upon in the text and it is not clear if Huxley makes the association knowingly. Fertile women, on the other hand, are represented by a circle, which, apart from its obvious genital associations, suggests zero, nothingness, hollow space, and passivity (11). Moreover, if we see it as our own symbol of women (Venus) minus the Christian cross, then, as men have gained divinity, women have had it taken from them. Other women who have been sterilized are designated by a question mark, as though suspicious or doubtful, and certainly something to snigger at. These "freemartins" do not constitute a third gender. They are still heterosexual and feminine, though, incidentally, since the latter comes from the root "to suckle," none of these childless women are in fact strictly "feminine." In any case, it is not clear if Huxley acknowledges a bias in the labeling of any of these categories (nor have I seen it outlined in any other critical works).

When it is a question of possessing knowledge or having an education, once again it is the men who appear to be in a superior position. In Huxley's account, women merely enter as narrative feeders, asking them for explanations. 'Why do the smoke-stacks have those things like balconies around them?' enquired Lenina. 'Phosphous recovery,' explained Henry telegraphically" (73), and he then goes on to lecture her at some length on this and other matters. Such interactions can again be explained by the fact that Huxley chooses to portray upper-class males addressing lower-class females. Instead of being scientists and leaders, the women we encounter perform auxiliary, service roles in nursing,[9] teaching, secretarial and factory work—the sort of jobs their contemporaries were in fact given in Huxley's society. These women therefore don't do science; they have science done to them. One area where technology has fundamentally altered female experience is motherhood, or, to use the industrial metaphor, "reproduction." In *Brave New World*, complete ectogenesis, not just in vitro fertilization, is the norm, which means that the site of reproduction is no longer the female body.

Again, why is this done? The ostensible reason, as Huxley presents it, is that ectogenesis facilitates conditioning and the efficient production of future citizens. This much is true. But could it also be attributed to a deeper masculine envy or fear, to the fulfillment of that ancient desire to create independently of the female, as in the Jewish Golem, the Christian "only-begotten" son, or Shelley's modern fantasy, Frankenstein? Despite the indisputable fact of the child emerging from the woman's body, for millennia male commentators have been quite ingenious at minimizing her role, for example, claiming that man is the active creator and woman only a passive container. Only in the 1870s, in fact, was it recognized that the woman's egg participated equally in fertilization.[10] But *Brave New World* takes us back to Aristotle, for now men (as scientists) can inform or design the fetus from mere feminine materiality. The biological mother is displaced and her awesome ability to create new life is safely curtailed. Male physicians or "pharmacrats" (Corea 2) were already beginning to monopolize childbirth in the West by the 1930s, but in Huxley's future society they have entirely appropriated the maternal function, reducing the female role to Lenina mechanically injecting fetuses in test tubes. In fact, motherhood is made taboo. The worst thing that can happen to a woman in this society is for her to become pregnant and carry a child to term (120, 153), and there is some evidence that Huxley was in sympathy with his dystopians on this point. The artificiality of the alternative procedure is meant to be shocking, but Huxley also found the intimacy of natural motherhood to be repugnant and even dangerous, especially for the child. Elsewhere in *Brave New World*, the traditional nuclear family is pictured as an unhealthy trap in which mothers are suffocating, domineering, and even sadistic (38, 41-42). Perhaps the fact that women lose some of this control through ectogenesis is not so regrettable in Huxley's view, though again female disempowerment is not his explicit focus.

Ectogenesis is possible because women who are fertile sell their ovaries to the State (3), a transaction that is not very different from prostitutes in our society who also sell parts of their bodies and is something that perhaps anticipates the commercial "stables" of surrogate mothers that have gone into business in recent years. When the women in *Brave New World* feel a void because they can never bear children themselves, they go to the male Dr. Wells (a glance back a H. G. Wells perhaps?) who cheerfully prescribes a chemical "Pregnancy Substitute" (37). But it is not clear that this hormonal treatment is, in fact, an adequate compensation. Without known offspring, these citizens obviously have no close relatives, and sex is generally separated not only from reproduction but also from love. Despite the hectic socializing, each citizen is totally alone.

Of course, one might argue that only release from motherhood allows a woman to achieve true equality and avoid the biological essentialism that ties the female identity to her reproductive capacities.[11] But this does not appear to be the case here. Separating sex and reproduction has not freed or empowered these women. Huxley rightly anticipated the profound social impact of the oral birth control pill, and he also assumed, again correctly, as it turned out, that women would bear the burden of contraception. In *Brave New World* 70 percent of females are sterilized and the remaining 30 percent are drilled on how to use the pill; yet men's natural processes are not modified in any way, an imbalance which is not remarked upon in the text. Neither the lot of men nor of women is meant to appear particularly attractive in this, as in any other, dystopia; but what this study has shown is that women are generally worse off than men and only in some instances is this a deliberate portrayal of something which earns Huxley's disapprobation.

Ape and Essence, Huxley's second alternative world, is not so much a technological as a posttechnological society. Published four years after the first denotation of an atomic bomb, this novel cum screenplay depicts the aftermath of a nuclear World War III and highlights the great irrationality of twentieth-century technology, that all our sophisticated "advances" are aimed at our destruction, that "the much touted technology, while it raises our standard of living, increases the probability of our violently dying" (40). Thanks to uncontrolled technological development to support idiocies like nationalism, the survivors of a nuclear holocaust have reverted back to horrible savagery. Generations later, there is long-term genetic damage, and it is with some sarcasm that Huxley introduces us to "a characteristic product of progressive technology—a hare-lipped Mongolian idiot" (80). Looking back, the narrator claims we should have foreseen that "men would be made so overwhelmingly bumptious by the miracles of their own technology that they would soon lose all sense of reality" (90). Now they are paying for it.

After the war, both technological products and know-how have largely been lost but not the desire to do exactly the same thing all over again. When the Botanist, Poole, arrives in neosavage California from a New Zealand which escaped most of the nuclear fallout, he is asked to explain his profession to the natives:

"A botanist is a man who knows about plants."
"War plants?" the Chief asks hopefully.
"No, no, just plants. Things with leaves and stalks and flowers...."

and so great is their disappointment that they propose to bury him alive on the spot (54). This is typical of the grim humor of the piece, but Huxley's serious point remains, that so long as technological knowledge is confined to a small caste of highly specialized experts then the knowledge base of our civilization is extremely fragile and can be shattered overnight. More generally, he is pointing to the gap between technological and ethical development,[12] to the sophistication of the means and the imbecility of the ends which are "ape-chosen" (35).

The Californians live in a pseudodemocracy that is actually a brutal hierarchy headed by what seems to be an all-male caste of administrators and eunuch priests, though again we learn of no explicit ruling which specifies that only men are to occupy superior positions. Here women are defined, or confined, by childbearing. Men capitalize on this function to punish them for giving birth to infants with genetic defects. Children are conceived during a short mating season of indiscriminate and casual sexual activity, after which biological fathers are not traced or held at all responsible. Male scientists such as Einstein, Faraday, Pasteur, and their military bosses, are named as ultimately responsible for the fallout that causes birth defects; nevertheless, women are used as scapegoats. As in *Brave New World*, motherhood is degrading, a curse. There is open hostility to women this time: it is part of the social structure and is condemned as such by Huxley. If, for example, a man finds a woman sexually attractive, she is blamed for bewitching him (an old idea in both Eastern and Western cultures) and it is she who is flogged (70). The violence against women is even more sadistic when young mothers are given just sufficient time to grow attached to their deformed infants before having to watch them he impaled on a butcher's knife in a public ritual (84). Catching the antifeminist strain of the Christian or Pauline Church, one character repeats the new catechism: "What is the Nature of Woman? Answer: Woman is the vessel of the Unholy Spirit, the source of all deformity, the enemy of the race...." (55). Indeed, women are commonly referred to as "Unholy Vessels," that is, passive receptacles or perhaps tools for man the technologist. Needless to say, none of this is seen as attractive by the narrator.

As in *Brave New World*, gender differences are preserved, even exaggerated, both in neosavage America and among the "civilized" New Zealanders, and again it works against females, though this is not the narrator's major concern, nor visit always explicit and decried. The scientist Poole, for example, is first seen as an unfortunately effeminate man crushed by a domineering mother, while his female colleague, Miss Hook, is another caricature of the spinsterish career woman, complete with horn-rimmed glasses and tweeds (38). Though she and other females are scientists in New Zealand, we note that Huxley assigns them the "softer" fields of botany and anthropology. The "hard" sciences are still a male preserve and the women passively look on as male scientists bullishly stake a claim for the role of their particular field in the disaster of the previous war (38). "Miss Hook" is simply out to catch her man, the reluctant Poole, but this is fixed when he meets an ultrafeminine—that is, helpless—junior and takes on a dominant, protective role. This provides for a happy ending when the conventional heterosexual roles are reinstated and he leads her into a new life. The narrator appears to approve of this, although Poole is playing a role not very different from that scoffed at earlier when one character fantasizes that he is "Flash the perpetual knight-errant to girls, not as they lamentably are, but as the idealists of the brassiere industry proclaim that they ought to be" (21).

Island, Huxley's final Utopia, shows how things could be if there was as much effort put into moral and spiritual, as into technological, advance.

Brave New World represents the peak of technological application and the human dependency it creates, and *Ape and Essence* represents the aftermath when this is suddenly wiped out; but in *Island* the Palanese keep firmly in mind that, as Huxley puts it, technology is made for man, not vice versa (*Island* 164). They make a point of getting away from Fordian specialization and piecemeal, conveyor-belt work. In fact, on this matter Huxley would pit Darwin against Ford, pointing out that human survival has depended precisely upon our lack of specialization. The islanders, therefore, live a varied life, and as part of their work they focus on the life sciences, on nurturing plants (living plants this time) and human life, rather than stimulating consumerism with technological luxuries (156). They also avoid heavy industry, which in Huxley's eyes is always associated with the twin horrors of militarization and centralization (169). As opposed to what I would call the &"cold" science of *Brave New World*, science here is "warm." "Cold" science is cut off from, and even hostile to, nature; in *Brave New World* this means aggression, competition, and triumph over natural processes. The talk may be of fertility rates, but the society as a whole is sterile. Notice the opening description of the technologists at work in *Brave New World*:

> Wintriness responded to wintriness. The overalls of the workers were white, their hands gloved with a pale corpse-coloured rubber. The light was frozen, dead, a ghost. (1)

The "warm" science of *Island*, on the other hand, aims to work with nature, and the result is accommodation rather than exploitation. This reflects Huxley's lifelong advocacy of a more ecological approach, long before this became fashionable. He drew on ancient ideas, Greek notions of hubris and nemesis as well as Eastern mysticism, to illustrate the universal importance of harmony and balance (*Island* 248-49). Some lessons, he felt, had already been learned in physics and chemistry, but he wanted to see these applied in other fields. For example, biology was now passing from an earlier passive phase of categorization into more active manipulation—as in genetic engineering—and Huxley felt it imperative to prevent this from going too "cold." He also advocated supplementing Western, material technology with the ancient psychological "technologies" of the East and working towards inner as well as external progress (*Island* 150-51).

But what of the progress of women's rights? Have these advanced? Huxley clearly found the outright hostility to women in the society of *Ape and Essence* distasteful, but in his utopia Huxley still seems unable to portray any scenario that radically departs from his own society's attitudes. In *Island* we encounter more important female characters, but the main narrative role for women, here as previously, is to induct the male outsider into the alternative society: here Susila inducts Will, before Lenina inducted John, and Loola inducted Poole. We know that the present social system in Pala was designed by two men, and men still appear to hold senior positions (as much as these can be determined), both political and religious. This time women can drive but are seen to do so only when men are physically unable (265). As in *Brave New World*, women are more often in assistant and nurturing roles. It is assumed that all nurses are female (77) and, though we see female teachers, the Under-Secretary for Education is a man (234). Once again Huxley is slipping into the stereotypes of his own society. The nearest we come to a woman in power, the Rani or Queen mother, is a heavily mocked and destructive figure. Due to patrilineal descent, she possesses no actual power and holds her position only as the widow of the previous ruler and mother of the next, but she is nevertheless seen as manipulative and threatening. Among the rest of the populace, monogamous marriages, in which the woman evidently takes her husband's name, appear to be the norm, but no details are given of how women balance outside careers and childrearing, though it appears they take on both. Huxley does not regard this as sufficiently important to discuss in any detail.

For the first time in his alternative worlds, homosexuality is accommodated. But meanwhile, heterosexual gender roles are still clearly differentiated, however much differences are now also seen as positive and complementary. "On top of being two hundred per cent male," the ideal man is now "almost fifty per cent sensitive-feminine" (229) which means that Huxley accepts gender stereotypes ("feminine" sensitivity) but now recommends some blending. With one couple, it is the wife's "brain" which is matched by her husband's "brawn" (220), but in two different generations we see the pattern of a marriage between an absorbed, intellectual male and a less intelligent, she is "intelligently simple" (206). As another wife explains to her husband, "I was always on tiptoes, always straining up towards the place where you were doing your work and your thinking and your reading" (40-41).

Again, the big change in female experience is in motherhood, which is at last seen as both positive and powerful. Huxley can now regard breastfeeding without flinching (218), and his hero, Will, learns to leave aside past associations of the womb and death (9) and embrace woman the life-giver. The romantic heroine we notice is a (widowed) mother and, through Susila, Will learns to reconcile the love and sexuality he previously divided between his wife and his mistress. Despite a phallic and powerful name, Will is actually emasculated and seeking a mother-figure-as-savior; this Susila is ready to provide along with her psychological first aid.

Now Huxley's focus is specifically on female as well as male happiness. In Will's previous experience—that is, our world—women are pictured as either angels, whores, or as passive, long-suffering wives and mothers. But on the island, we are assured that all women are much happier. Perhaps, for one thing, this is due to their greater say in matters of reproduction, a development that is regarded as beneficial for women and for society. State-issued contraceptives for both men and women presumably allow women some say on whether or not to have a child in the first place, though apparently only within marriage (92). Artificial insemination with donor sperm (A.I.D.) also enables them, no doubt in consultation with their husbands, to select the genetic makeup of their offspring. In such cases, donor sperm comes from a bank and the process involves no sexual impregnation, which means that there is still sexual, if not biological, fidelity between husband and wife. Nevertheless, this procedure does displace the husband as biological father and thereby undermines direct patriarchal descent. Apparently the Palanese men don't have any objections to this but happily stand aside so their wives' children can have a good genetic inheritance (220-21), whereas it is worth remembering that in our society, as late as 1963, A.I.D. was regarded as adulterous and grounds for divorce (Corea 40). It may be that women are happier in *Island* also because Huxley has not neglected the female orgasm. The "yoga of love,"which is part of Palanese religious practice, is apparently very satisfying for the female partner, giving her both sexual and spiritual equal opportunity (98)! Evidently, women have gained some ground in this utopia, but there is still no direct indication that this greater control is paralleled in Pala's formal politics.

And what of the scientific sphere? Is the "warm" science I referred to earlier seen as more feminine than the scientific attitude found in *Brave New World*? The Palanese appear to have modified the West's seventeenth-century mechanization of nature, realigning themselves with an older, also Eastern, attitude which sees nature as vital and organic, a worldview that has indeed been associated with the feminine.[13] They are also more interested in the "soft" than the traditionally masculinist, "hard" sciences, and their methodology is more holistic and nurturing than destructive, again qualities conventionally associated with the feminine. However, there is no evidence that Huxley makes these associations or that he invokes the gendered polarity of nature (feminine) and science/ culture (masculine) in any of these works.

What we have seen in each of these societies is that technology often radically affects women's experience but appears to be controlled by men and that, whatever their society, men and women appear to enjoy equal political status in principle; but this is not what emerges from Huxley's portrayal. Even when attempting to better the female lot, he repeatedly adopts the sexist norms of his own society without even being aware of it. It is not a question of realism, for one of the obvious features of utopias is that they need not reflect anything of the current status quo; indeed, their agenda is generally to radically alter it. Nevertheless, though *Island* does show some improvement of the female position compared to the two previous dystopias and compared to Huxley's own society, it is not as alternative a world as one might expect. This reflects the lack of serious attention to the position of women in the mainstream (or male-stream) utopian tradition. Even authors who in theory advocate equal opportunity for women don't appear to take the issue seriously enough to follow through and portray this in practice. In fictional utopias it is, quite legitimately, enactment which counts. This is no mere detail—rather, mere details are significant, for what is depicted, what is worked out in detail, is what most impresses the reader. One thinks of Edward Bellamy's hugely influential *Looking Backward* (1888) where women have theoretical opportunities that are simply not convincingly realized in practice. Bellamy's women supposedly have full-time careers outside the home; yet in practice, the heroine, Miss Leete, appears to be very little different from her Victorian ancestors, being occupied with nothing more than occasional shopping trips or flower arranging at the breakfast table. At least William Morris was more consistent when, writing in response to Bellamy a few years later, he came right out and said that women prefer these domestic tasks and should continue to perform them (234).

In Huxley's works, women have as much opportunity relative to men— at least in theory—in the dystopia *Brave New World* as in the eutopia *Island*; one social arrangement may in its entirety be obviously preferable to the other, but a woman's relative position does not greatly alter. In other words, it is clear that the fate of women alone does not define these societies as eutopian or dystopian, and it is not something to which Huxley pays a great deal of attention. Only on a few occasions does he suggest that women in *Brave New World* are treated differently or more unfairly than the male citizen. In the area of female rights, one might say that Huxley sins more by omission than intention. Perhaps this makes it the more damning; for all his ability to think differently on the technological front, in the underlying sexual politics the more things change, the more they stay the same.

NOTES

[1] Actually, it would be unfair, though common, to label Wells a facile or die-hard optimist. Nevertheless, he was very offended by *Brave New World*, seeing it as a betrayal both of science and the future. See Gerald Heard 57.

[2] Although Huxley found some solace in reading Henry Ford's *My Life and Work* after viewing the poverty of India (*Jesting Pilate* 213-14), he generally loathed Ford and all he stood for. See, for example, *Music at Night* 127-28.

[3] This was established at the International Conference on Time in Paris. For the socio-political ramifications of this and other technological innovations, see Kern.

[4] Huxley stayed with the Haldanes while at Oxford and no doubt got many of his ideas for *Brave New World* from J. B. S. Haldane's *Daedalus: Or Science and the Future*. For confirmation of this, see *Proper Studies* 278.

[5] In Britain women aged thirty and over got the vote in 1918 and were accorded equal voting rights with men (aged twenty-one and over) in 1928.

[6] "Uncorseted, her friendly bust / Gives promise of pneumatic bliss." T. S. Eliot, "Whispers of Immortality."

[7] This does not necessarily reflect Huxley's own views. Indeed, it is thought that Huxley's wife Maria was a lesbian. See Dunaway 70.

[8] For an introduction to feminist studies of science, see Ruth Bleier, Donna Haraway, Sandra Harding, Evelyn Fox Keller, Carolyn Merchant, and Nancy Tuana.

[9] Interestingly, even when Huxley avoids assigning a gender to the nurses he mentions, in my experience students tend to assume they have been designated as female.

[10] For an account of male trivialization of the female's role in reproduction, see Nancy Tuana, "The Weaker Seed: The Sexist Bias of Reproductive Theory," 147-71.

[11] For example, Firestone sets the "freeing of women from the tyranny of their reproductive biology" as a primary aim in any feminist revolution (223).

[12] See also *Literature and Science* 92-93; *Letters* 578-79; *Time Must Have a Stop* 274, 78-79.

13 For an account of the seventeenth-century replacement of a more feminine worldview with masculinist modern science, see Keller and Merchant.

Works Cited

Bellamy, Edward. *Looking Backward: 2000-1887*. Ed. Cecelia Tichi. 1888. New York: Penguin, 1982.

Bleier, Ruth, ed. *Feminist Approaches to Science*. New York: Pergamon, 1986.

Corea, Gena. *The Mother Machine: Reproductive Technologies from Artificial Insemination to Artificial Wombs*. New York: Harper, 1985.

Dunaway, David King. *Huxley in Hollywood*. New York: Harper, 1989.

Eliot, T. S. "Whispers of Immortality." *Collected Poems 1909-1935*. New York: Harcourt, 1936. 61.

Firestone, Shulamith. *The Dialectic of Sex*. New York: Morrow, 1970.

Ford, Henry, and Samuel Crowther. *My Life and Work*. New York: Doubleday, 1922.W

Haldane, J. B. S. *Daedalus: Or Science and the Future*. London: Paul, 1924.

Haraway, Donna. *Primate Visions: Gender, Race and Nature in the World of Modern Science*. New York: Routledge, 1989.

Harding, Sandra. *The Science Question in Feminism*. Ithaca: Cornell UP, 1986.

Heard, Gerald. "The Poignant Prophet." *Kenyon Review* 27 (Winter 1965): 49-70.

Huxley, Aldous. *Ape and Essence: A Novel*. 1949. London: Chatto and Windus, 1966.

———. *Brave New World*. 1932. New York: Harper, 1969.

———. *Island: A Novel*. London: Chatto and Windus, 1962.

———. *Jesting Pilate*. 1926. London: Chatto and Windus, 1948.

———. *Letters*. Ed. Grover Smith. London: Chatto and Windus, 1969.

———. *Literature and Science*. London: Chatto and Windus, 1963.

———. *Music at Night*. 1931. London: Chatto and Windus, 1970.

———. *Proper Studies*. 1927. London: Chatto and Windus, 1957.

————. *Time Must Have a Stop*. London: Chatto and Windus, 1945.

Keller, Evelyn Fox. *Reflections on Gender and Science*. New Haven: Yale UP, 1985.

Kern, Stephen. *The Culture of Time and Space 1880-1918*. Cambridge: Harvard UP, 1983.

Kuhn, Thomas S. *The Structure of Scientific Revolutions*. 1962. Chicago: U of Chicago P, 1970.

Kumar, Krishan. *Utopia and Anti-Utopia in Modern Times*. Oxford: Basil Blackwell, 1987.

McLaughlin, Loretta. *The Pill, John Rock, and the Church: The Biography of a Revolution*. Boston: Little, Brown, 1982.

Merchant, Carolyn. *The Death of Nature: Women, Ecology, and the Scientific Revolution*. San Francisco: Harper, 1980.

Morris, William. *News from Nowhere and Selected Writings and Designs*. 1891. New York: Penguin, 1984.

Plimpton, George, ed. *Writers at Work: The Paris Review Interviews*. 2nd series. New York: Viking, 1963.

Shelley, Mary. *Frankenstein: Or the Modern Prometheus*. Ed. Maurice Hindle. 1818. New York: Penguin, 1985.

Tuana, Nancy, ed. *Feminism and Science*. Bloomington: Indiana UP, 1989.

Wells, H. G. *Men Like Gods*. New York: Macmillan, 1923.

Chronology

1894	Aldous Leonard Huxley born in Godalming, Surrey, England, 26 July.
1903	Attends Hillside School.
1908	Enters Eton on scholarship. Mother dies.
1910	Nearly blinded by eye infection. Leaves Eton.
1913	Vision improves. Enters Balliol College, Oxford.
1914	Brother Trev commits suicide.
1915	Joins literary circle at Garsington Manor House under the sponsorship of Lady Ottoline Morrell. Meets D.H. Lawrence and T.S. Eliot.
1916	Publishes *The Burning Wheel*, his first volume of poems.
1917	Teaches at Eton. Works at the Air Ministry.
1919	Marries Maria Nys, a Belgian refugee.
1920	Publishes *Limbo*, a collection of short stories.
1921	Publishes *Crome Yellow*, his first novel.
1922	Publishes *Mortal Coils*, short stories.
1923	Publishes *Antic Hay*, a novel. Moves to Italy.
1925	Publishes *Those Barren Leaves*, a novel. Starts a world tour.
1926	Publishes *Jesting Pilate*, a travel book. Renews friendship with D.H. Lawrence.
1928	Publishes *Point Counter Point*, a novel.

1929	Publishes *Do What You Will*, his first major collection of essays.
1930	Buys house at Sanary in southern France. D.H. Lawrence dies.
1931	Publishes *Music at Night*, collection of essays.
1932	Publishes *Brave New World*.
1934	Travels in Central America and southern Mexico. Publishes *Beyond the Mexique Bay*, collection of essays.
1935	Takes part in H.R.L. Sheppard's Peace Movement. Delivers lectures on peace.
1936	Publishes *Eyeless in Gaza*, a novel.
1937	Publishes *Ends and Means*. Moves to southern California. Meets Swami Prabhavananda and joins Vendanta movement of California.
1939	Publishes *After Many a Summer Dies the Swan*, a novel. Meets Christopher Isherwood.
1940	Starts writing scenarios for Hollywood films. Writes the screenplay for the film version of Jane Austen's *Pride and Prejudice*, starring Laurence Olivier and Greer Garson.
1941	Publishes *Grey Eminence*, a historical novel.
1944	Publishes *Time Must Have a Stop*, a novel.
1945	Publishes *The Perennial Philosophy*, a collection of essays.
1948	Publishes *Apes and Essence*, a novel.
1950	Publishes *Themes and Variation*, a collection of essays.
1952	Publishes *The Devils of Loudon*, a historical novel.
1953	First starts experimenting with psychedelic drugs, like mescaline.
1954	Publishes *The Doors of Perception*, based on his experiences with drugs.
1955	Huxley's wife, Maria, dies. Publishes *The Genius and the Goddess*.
1956	Marries Laura Archera.
1958	Publishes *Brave New World Revisited*, a discussion of his earlier dystopia.
1959	Receives Award from the American Academy of Letters.
1960	Diagnosed with cancer of the tongue.

1961	California home burns down. Papers and manuscripts destroyed.
1962	Elected a Companion of Literature of the British Royal Society of Literature (one of ten such positions). Publishes *Island*, a utopian novel.
1963	Dies in California, November 22.

Contributors

HAROLD BLOOM is Sterling Professor of the Humanities at Yale University and Henry W. and Albert A. Berg Professor of English at the New York University Graduate School. He is the author of over 20 books, including *Shelly's Mythmaking* (1959), *The Visionary Company* (1961), *Blake's Apocalypse* (1963), *Yeats* (1970), *A Map of Misreading* (1975), *Kabbalah and Criticism* (1975), *Agon: Toward a Theory of Revisionism* (1982), *The American Religion* (1992), *The Western Canon* (1994), and *Omens of Millennium: The Gnosis of Angels, Dreams, and Resurrection* (1996). *The Anxiety of Influence* (1973) sets forth Professor Bloom's provocative theory of the literary relationships between the great writers and their predecessors. His most recent books include *Shakespeare: The Invention of the Human*, a 1998 National Book Award finalist, and *How to Read and Why*, which was published in 2000. In 1999, Professor Bloom received the prestigious American Academy of Arts and Letters Gold Medal for Criticism.

WILLIAM M. JONES is a literary scholar and critic whose work has appeared in such journals as *The Western Humanities Review*.

PETER BOWERING is a respected essayist and academic. His published work includes *Aldous Huxley: a Study of the Major Novels*.

HAROLD H. WATTS has been a professor of English at Purdue University. His critical essays have appeared in such journals as *The Kenyon Review* and *The Sewanee Review*. He is also the author of the critical volume *Ezra Pound*.

JEROME MECKIER is a scholar and an essayist whose published work includes *Aldous Huxley: Satire and Structure*.

GEORGE WOODCOCK has been a prominent poet, critic, professor, editor, biographer, historian and essayist. He has published numerous books including *The Crystal Spirit: A Study of George Orwell* and *The Anarchist Prince* (a biography of Peter Kropotkin).

PHILIP THODY has been the Chair of French Literature at Leeds University. He has written several critical and biographical volumes on influential writers, including *Sartre* and *Aldous Huxley: a biographical introduction*.

ROBERT S. BAKER has been a professor of English at the University of Wisconsin at Madison. He is the author of *The Dark Historic Page: Social Satire and Historicism in the Novels of Aldous Huxley, 1921-1939* and *Brave New World: History, Science, and Dystopia*.

PETER EDGERLY FIRCHOW has been an active educator and critic. He is the author of *Aldous Huxley: Satirist and Novelist* and *The End of Utopia: A Study of Aldous Huxley's* Brave New World.

JUNE DEERY is a scholar and essayist who has done significant research in gender theory. Her work has appeared in such journals as *Extrapolation*.

Bibliography

Adorno, Theodor W. *Negative Dialectics*. New York: Continuum Publishing Company, 1987.

Alderidge, Alexandra. *The Scientific World View in Dystopia*. Ann Arbor: UMI Research Press, 1984.

Atkinson, R.F. *Knowledge and Explanation in History: An Introduction to the Philosophy of History*. Ithaca: Cornell University Press, 1978.

Baker, Robert S. *The Dark Historic Page: Social Satire and Historicism in the Novels of Aldous Huxley, 1921-1939*. Madison: University of Wisconsin Press, 1982.

Bedford, Sybille. *Aldous Huxley: A Biography*. New York: Alfred A. Knopf/Harper and Row, 1974.

Beetham, David. *Bureaucracy*. Minneapolis: University of Minnesota Press, 1987.

Bleich, David. *Utopia: The Psychology of a Cultural Fantasy*. Ann Arbor: UMI Research Press, 1984.

Brander, Laurence. *Aldous Huxley: A Critical Study*. Lewisburg: Bucknell University Press, 1970.

Brown, E.J. *Brave New World, 1984, and We: An Essay on Anti-Utopia*. Ann Arbor: Ardis, 1976.

Carr, Edward Hallett. *The Twenty Years Crisis, 1919-1939*. London: MacMillan, 1954.

Daiches, David. "Aldous Huxley," *The Novel and the Modern World*. Chicago: University of Chicago Press, 1939.

Firchow, Peter Edgerly. *Aldous Huxley: Satirist and Novelist*. Minneapolis: University of Minnesota Press, 1972.

————. *The End of Utopia: A Study of Aldous Huxley's Brave New World*. Lewisburg: Bucknell University Press, 1984.

Ferns, C.S. *Aldous Huxley: Novelist*. London: Athlone Press, 1980.

Fourier, Charles. *Design for Utopia*. Ed. Charles Gide. New York: Schocken Books, 1971.

Glicksberg, Charles I. Aldous Huxley: Art and Mysticism," *Prairie Schooner* XXVII (Winter, 1953): 344-53.

Haldane, J.B.S. "Biological Possibilities for the Human Species in the Next Ten Thousand Years," in *Man and His Future*. Ed. Gordon Wolstenholme. London: J.A. Churchill, 1963.

Henderson, Alexander. *Aldous Huxley*. London: Chatto & Windus, 1935.

Holmes, Charles M. *Aldous Huxley and the Way to Reality*. Bloomington: University of Indiana Press, 1970.

Jameson, Frederic. *The Political Unconscious: Narrative as a Socially Symbolic Act*. Ithaca: Cornell University Press, 1981.

Kateb, George. *Utopia and Its Enemies*. Glencoe: Free Press, 1963.

Mannheim, Karl. *Ideology and Utopia: An Introduction to the Sociology of Knowledge*. London: Routledge and Kegan Paul, 1966.

Manuel, F.E. and F.P. *Utopian Thought in the Western World*. Cambridge: Harvard University Press, 1979.

May, Keith. *Aldous Huxley*. New York: Barnes and Noble, 1972.

Mazlish, Bruce. *The Riddle of History: The Great Speculators from Vico to Freud*. New York: Harper and Row, 1955.

Meckier, Jerome. *Aldous Huxley: Satire and Structure*. London: Chatto and Windus, 1969.

Nisbet, Robert. *History of the Idea of Progress*. New York: Basic Books, 1980.

Quina, James H. "The Philosophical Phases of Aldous Huxley," *College English* XXIII (May, 1962): 636-41.

Robert, John H. "Huxley and Lawrence," *Virginia Quarterly Review* XIII (Autumn, 1937): 546-57.

Shklar, Judith N. *After Utopia*. Princeton, N.J.: Princeton University Press, 1957.

Snow, Melinda. "The Gray Parody in *Brave New World*," *Papers on Language and Literature 13* (Winter 1977): 85-88.

Spender, Stephen. *The Destructive Element: A Study of Modern Writers and Beliefs*. London: Jonathan Cape, 1935.

Thody, Philip. *Aldous Huxley: A Biographical Introduction*. New York: Charles Scribner's Sons, 1973.

Watt, Donald, ed. *Aldous Huxley: The Critical Heritage*. London: Routledge and Kegan Paul, 1975.

Watt, Donald. "The Manuscript Revisions of *Brave New World*," *Journal of English and German Philology* 77 (July 1978): 367-82.

Watts, Harold. *Aldous Huxley*. New York: Twayne, 1959.

White, Hayden. *Metahistory: The Historical Imagination in Nineteenth-CenturyEurope*. Baltimore: Johns Hopkins University Press, 1973.

Woodcock, George. *Dawn and the Darkest Hour: A Study of Aldous Huxley*. New York: Viking, 1972.

Acknowledgments

"The Iago of *Brave New World*" by William M. Jones from *The Western Humanities Review*, Vol. XV, No. 3 (Summer, 1961): 275-278. © 1961 by *The Western Humanities Review*. Reprinted by Permission.

"*Brave New World* (1932)" by Peter Bowering from *Aldous Huxley: a Study of the Major Novels*: 98-113. © 1968 by Peter Bowering. Reprinted by Permission.

"*Brave New World*" by Harold H. Watts from *Aldous Huxley*: 72-84. © 1969 by Twayne Publishers, Inc. Reprinted by Permission of the Gale Group.

"Utopian Counterpoint and the Compensatory Dream" by Jerome Meckier from *Aldous Huxley: Satire and Structure*: 175-205. © 1969 by Jerome Meckier. Reprinted by Permission.

"Destructive Encounters" by George Woodcock from *Dawn and the Darkest Hour: A Study of Aldous Huxley*: 163-181. © 1972 by George Woodcock. Reprinted by Permission.

"*Brave New World*" by Philip Thody from *Huxley: a biographical introduction*: 48-60. © 1973 by Philip Thody. Reprinted by Permission.

"*Brave New World:* Huxley's Dystopian Dilemma" by Robert S. Baker from *The Dark Historic Page: Social Satire and Historicism in the Novels of Aldous Huxley 1921-1939*: 135-145. © 1982 by The University of Wisconsin Press. Reprinted by Permission.

"The End of Utopia: A Study of Aldous Huxley's *Brave New World*" by Peter Edgerly Firchow © 1984 by Bucknell University Press. Reprinted by Permission of Associated University of Presses.

"History and Psychology in the World State" by Robert S. Baker from *Brave New World: History, Science, and Dystopia*: 88-99. © 1990 by G.K. Hall & Co. Reprinted by Permission.

"*Brave New World*: Overview" by George Woodcock from *Reference Guide to English Literature*, 2nd ed., edited by D.L. Kirkpatrick. © 1991 by St. James Press. Reprinted by Permission.

"Technology and Gender in Aldous Huxley's Alternative (?) Worlds" by June Deery from *Extrapolation*, Vol. 33, No. 3, (Fall, 1992): 258-73. © 1992 by *Extrapolation*. Reprinted by Permission of the Kent State University Press.

Index